The Teaching

of

Modern Foreign Languages

and the

Training of Teachers

The Teaching

of

Modern Foreign Languages

and the

Training of Teachers

By

KARL BREUL

Litt.D. (Cambridge), Ph.D. (Berlin)

Schröder Professor of German in the University of Cambridge

FOURTH EDITION
Revised and Enlarged

Cambridge

at the University Press

1913

CAMBRIDGE
UNIVERSITY PRESS

University Printing House, Cambridge CB2 8BS, United Kingdom

Cambridge University Press is part of the University of Cambridge.

It furthers the University's mission by disseminating knowledge in the pursuit of education, learning and research at the highest international levels of excellence.

www.cambridge.org
Information on this title: www.cambridge.org/9781316601785

© Cambridge University Press 1913

First edition 1898
Second edition 1899
Third edition 1906
Fourth edition 1909
Reprinted 1913
First paperback edition 2015

A catalogue record for this publication is available from the British Library

ISBN 978-1-316-60178-5 Paperback

PREFACE

THE paper 'on the teaching of modern foreign languages' was first read, in the Lent Term of 1895, to the students of the 'Cambridge Training College for Women Teachers' and was twice repeated, with but a few alterations, in subsequent years. It was also read, by the request of the Syndicate, to the students attending the Cambridge University Extension Courses in August 1896.

The lectures were originally intended to form an Introduction to some criticism lessons of modern language lessons given by the students of the Training College, and the principles set forth in the lectures were at once practically applied in the detailed criticism of the lessons heard. The lectures were intended to be above all suggestive and stimulating, but no attempt could be made to discuss in full the views either of the old school of language teachers and examiners who are hostile to any reform or of some modern extremists.

A few slight alterations were introduced and some references to recent literature on the subject added when the lectures were revised for the Press, but, apart from these exceptions, they are substantially printed as they were first written in the Christmas Vacation of 1894.

A paper 'on the training of teachers of modern foreign languages,' read in April 1894 to the College of Preceptors (printed in the *Educational Times*, May 1894, and reprinted by Professor Viëtor's special request in *Die Neueren Sprachen*

II. 424 sqq., 585 sqq.), supplements in several respects the views set forth in these lectures and may be read in connection with them.

The essay describing the contents of a well-equipped 'reference library of a school teacher of German' is a revised and enlarged reprint from the *Modern Language Quarterly* II. It was thought that many teachers would like to have it as a useful appendix to the first paper.

The author is anxious to tender his heartiest thanks to Dr Henry Jackson of Trinity College, Professor G. C. Moore Smith, M.A., of the Firth College, Sheffield, and the Rev. W. A. Cox, M.A., of St John's College, who kindly read through the lectures and contributed some valuable suggestions.

The author is convinced that many important changes are needed in our present system of Modern Language teaching and examining; he believes that many teachers share this conviction and are ready to consider new problems in con nection with their teaching and to take part in the necessary re-modelling of the system. It is hoped that to such teachers the present pamphlet will be acceptable. The outlook seems promising. Modern Languages are at last beginning to re ceive in this country the attention to which the subject is entitled not only by its practical usefulness but still more by its intrinsic value as an important element in a truly liberal education.

K. B.

Englemere,
 Cambridge,
  October, 1898.

PREFACE TO THE SECOND EDITION

THE fact that the first edition of the present little book was sold out in the course of a few months is a most encouraging sign of the rapidly growing interest of teachers and students in the problems connected with modern language teaching. There was neither time nor need to introduce any important changes into the new edition, but the whole book has been very carefully revised and the lists of books and pamphlets on modern language teaching have been considerably enlarged. This was chiefly due to the fact that several excellent contributions to important questions of method had quite recently been published. Among those who kindly contributed a number of valuable suggestions for the revision of the book the author wishes to mention, with due gratitude, the names of W. G. Lipscomb and of Walter Rippmann.

K. B.

ENGLEMERE,
    CAMBRIDGE,
        Easter, 1899.

PREFACE TO THE THIRD EDITION

IN this third edition I have not only carefully revised and largely added to the lectures printed in the previous editions, with a view to bringing them up to date and of making them as useful and suggestive as lies in my power—but I have added to them an enlarged reprint of my lecture 'on the training of teachers of modern languages' which was originally given twelve years ago to members of the College of Preceptors. The lectures 'on the teaching of modern languages,' and those 'on the training of modern language teachers,' supplement each other and may well be read together. The last chapter is an improved reprint of my sketch of an ideal 'reference library for a school teacher of German' which I hope will be found as widely useful by young teachers in the future as it has been helpful to others in the past. A few slight cases of overlapping in the various chapters of the book could not, from the nature of the subject, be altogether avoided, and will, I hope, not be felt to be very troublesome. A full index at the end of the book will enable the reader readily to obtain information on any question discussed in any of the lectures.

A kind reviewer of the original edition expressed the hope that in a revised edition I might unite the various lectures into one comprehensive treatise, and map out in it a complete course of modern language, or German, study from its beginnings up to and including the University curriculum.

For more than one reason I have not been able to comply with this wish. One is that, even if I had wished to do so, the very limited time which has been at my disposal during recent years has prevented me from embarking on so laborious an undertaking. I also believe that part of the stimulus given by my lectures has been due to the somewhat easy and unceremonious form in which the subject was treated. But above all I feel very strongly that a detailed scheme of teaching foreign languages in schools ought to be elaborated only by a practical school teacher. I have for many years followed the teaching of modern languages, more especially of German, in this country and abroad with much interest; I have had, as an examiner, exceptional opportunities of studying the results obtained by all kinds of teachers in our various secondary schools for boys and girls; I have thus been able to make many interesting observations and comparisons, and feel quite confident as to the general principles according to which the teaching in our schools ought to be conducted—but it would be presumptuous on my part to advise practical school teachers about points of detail. I sincerely hope that before long a comprehensive book on the subject may be produced by one of our leading teachers. Till then I wish to call attention to the excellent American book of E. W. Bagster-Collins (see p. 118) in which the teaching of German has been very ably and fully treated. I am myself at the present moment preparing a book on the higher study of German at universities[1], which I hope may prove a useful continuation to a book on the school teaching of German and meet a real want in our educational literature.

Many important steps in advance have been made in this country during the last seven years with regard to the teaching

---

[1] It will be considerably fuller than Heinz Hungerland's recent pamphlet ' Das wissenschaftliche Studium der deutschen Sprache und Literatur. Ein Wegweiser für Studierende.' Lund and Heidelberg, 1906.

of modern languages and the facilities given for the training of teachers.   At the University of Oxford the much needed Honour School of modern languages has at last been established and some provision at least been made for a higher scientific teaching.   At the University of London two professors and three readers have been appointed with a view to creating in London a school of German, and it is hoped that French will soon find the same encouragement.   At Cambridge, where the Medieval and Modern Languages Tripos has now for over twenty years been an instrument of training many excellent teachers and professors for our schools and colleges, two fellowships have of late been given to modern language men. At some of the newer universities lectureships have been raised to the dignity of professorships, assistants have been appointed, and at Bangor a lectureship in French and German has been fitly split up and changed into a professorship of French and (for the present) a lectureship in German.   At Edinburgh it is hoped to change before long the existing lectureships in French and German into professorships. Several headmasterships have of late been given to modern language men.   The numbers of the members of the Modern Language Association have been steadily increasing, and the Association is now bringing out two periodicals, one concerned with the higher study, and one with the teaching of modern languages, apart from the interest shown in the subject, not only by the 'Journal of Education' (which has always been friendly and encouraging), but also by its younger contemporary the 'School World.'   The number of travelling scholarships for teachers and students has been increased.   The scheme of international correspondence of pupils and of teachers, and the quite recent important scheme of an official exchange of teachers between England on the one hand and France and Prussia on the other, are sure to bear good fruit.   Oral examinations and improved methods of teaching are now found in many universities and schools.   Scholars' and teachers' libraries, wall-maps, phonographs, and other apparatus are to some extent beginning to be provided at several of the best schools. Many important questions as to the methods of teaching and examining have been discussed at the General Meetings of the Modern Language Association, where many opportunities for a useful interchange of views and experiences were given to individual members. Successful interchanges of visits between English and French teachers of modern languages have taken place in recent years.

If thus it is clear that much has been done during the last seven years, I still know very well that much more remains to be achieved. I have no doubt that now, when so many able and enthusiastic teachers, men and women, are at work under improved conditions and with many opportunities of comparing notes with English and foreign colleagues, the methods of modern language teaching will soon be further improved, the results obtained be still more satisfactory, the status of duly qualified teachers be raised, and the great importance of the new humanities for a liberal education of the rising generation be more fully and effectively recognised.

My best thanks are due to some friends and former pupils of mine for helping me, by sending suggestions and otherwise, in the preparation of this new edition and in bringing it in every respect up to date. They are Professors A. W. Schüddekopf, Ph.D., H. G. Atkins, M.A., Walter Rippmann, M.A., and Miss Josephine Burne, late scholar of Newnham College.

K. B.

10 CRANMER ROAD,
  CAMBRIDGE,
    August, 1906.

PREFACE TO THE FOURTH EDITION

THE short space of time that has elapsed between the publication of the third and the preparation of the fourth edition is a most satisfactory proof of the increasing interest that is now taken in everything pertaining to the furtherance of the thorough study and efficient teaching of German and French in Great Britain. This gratifying fact has encouraged me to revise my little book again very carefully, to increase it not inconsiderably, and to bring it up to date in every respect as far as lay in my power. I hope that it may once more prove useful to many students and teachers, and, in some parts, also to educationists and members of local Education Committees who have officially to deal with modern languages.

Since August 1906, when my last preface was written, the University of Oxford has established the Taylorian Professorship of German and will probably before long found a chair of Romance by the side of existing Lectureships in German and French. The Chancellor of the University of Cambridge has included a fuller provision for Modern Languages among the most pressing needs of this University, whose Medieval and Modern Languages Tripos will within a few months be able to claim the honour of having trained modern language teachers and scholars for a quarter of a century. In Scotland earnest endeavours are being made, at one at least of the four Universities, to raise the lectureships of German and French to the dignity of professorships. The number of members of the 'Modern Language Association' is steadily increasing, and its influence is beginning to make itself widely felt.

There remains to me the pleasant duty of thanking a number of friends and former pupils for kindly helping me, by sending suggestions and otherwise, in the preparation of this new edition. They are Professors H. G. Fiedler, M.A., Ph.D., Arwid Johannson, M.A., Ph.D., Walter Rippmann, M.A., Mr Francis E. Sandbach, M.A., Ph.D., Mr G. Morier Hinde, M.A., Miss Hinde, and Mr W. S. Montgomerie, B.A., formerly scholar of St John's College and now Englischer Lektor in the University of Greifswald. I feel especially obliged to Miss Bessie H. A. Robson, M.A., Lecturer on Phonetics in the Provincial Training College, Edinburgh, who, in addition to several useful suggestions, kindly contributed, at my request, the paragraphs on 'books for young German readers, picture books and decorative wall pictures' (pages 154—6), of which subjects she has made a special study.

K. B.

10 CRANMER ROAD,
   CAMBRIDGE,
      Easter, 1909.

CONTENTS

		PAGE
I.	THE TEACHING OF MODERN FOREIGN LANGUAGES IN OUR SECONDARY SCHOOLS . .	1–85
	a. General part	1–60
	b. Special part : The Teaching of German.	61–85
II.	THE TRAINING OF MODERN LANGUAGE TEACHERS	86–113
III.	BIBLIOGRAPHICAL APPENDIX	114–128
IV.	THE REFERENCE LIBRARY OF A SCHOOL TEACHER OF GERMAN	129–164
V.	APPENDIX	165–171
	INDEX	172–176

THE TEACHING
OF MODERN FOREIGN LANGUAGES
IN OUR SECONDARY SCHOOLS

THE subject which I propose to discuss in these lectures can certainly not be likened to a smooth and flower-strewn path. If it is not exactly beset with thorns, it may yet appear to outsiders to be stony, dull, and probably devoid of those beautiful vistas which those who unweariedly climb the upward path have a reasonable hope of beholding in the end. Moreover my lectures must of necessity be somewhat technical, and the limited time at my disposal strictly forbids me to enter some of the by-paths from the main road, which often afford no small amount of amusement beside material for very serious reflection. One of these digressions would be a short sketch of the early days of modern language teaching, a discussion of the old quaint 'babees bookes' or 'bookes of Curtesy' which sometimes combined teaching of modern languages with teaching of good manners[1]. Another digression would be a discussion of the results frequently obtained by the

[1] See my edition of the fifteenth century poem 'The Boke of Curtesy' in *Englische Studien*, IX (1885), pages 51 and foll., and compare R. Dyboski in '*Bausteine*,' *Zeitschrift für neuenglische Wortforschung*, I (1906), 335 sqq. and his brief notice in Vol. CI of the 'Early English Text Society, Extra Series,' London, 1907, p. xli. Compare also W. Viëtor, 'Die Methodik des Neusprachlichen Unterrichts,' Leipzig, 1902, pp. 4 sqq. (Vom Mittelalter zur Neuzeit).

present system of modern language teaching in some of our Secondary Schools. It has been my lot for many years to make from time to time a careful study of that very remarkable and ever increasing part of educational literature which is known to the scholastic world by the high-sounding name of 'examination papers.' From the questions asked in these papers and the answers to them one may gather some ideas as to the aims and results of modern language teaching—here I refer especially to the teaching of German and French—in our Secondary Schools, and if I were to tabulate my experiences, the results would in some cases be very curious. In what way, do you think, must a girl have been taught, in what spirit must she have read that great masterpiece of Goethe, his lofty play 'Iphigenie,' when in answer to my question 'Why do we take an interest in the character of Iphigenie?' she candidly writes 'Because Iphigenia is the heroine of the play which we had to get up for this examination'? But I must abstain from telling anecdotes which are none the less interesting for the fact that they are absolutely true.

Again, I can only allude in passing to the history of the 'reform movement' in the teaching of foreign tongues, the leading ideas of which were set forth lucidly and forcibly by Professor Wilhelm Viëtor (of Marburg) in his famous pamphlet : '*Quousque tandem! Der Sprachunterricht muss umkehren*[1].' This revolutionary little treatise was written in this country in 1882, and though not absolutely the first work in which a reform of modern language teaching was advocated, was yet the first which, by virtue of its shortness, terseness, and common sense, produced a great stir among modern language teachers. Since that date very many books and papers have been written *pro* and *contra*, in Germany and in other countries,

[1] See p. 124, under 80. Cp. also W. Viëtor, 'Wissenschaft und Praxis in der neueren Philologie,' Speech delivered Jan. 27, 1899, reprinted in *Die Neueren Sprachen*, VII. 1 (April), 1899, and also p. 124, Nos. 81 and 82.

most of them advocating a more or less radical reform of the old system of teaching in the spirit of the so-called 'direct,' 'analytic,' or 'imitative' method. The 'New Method,' or 'Neuere Richtung,' has been fully developed in Germany, and its main principles have been deservedly adopted by a small band of energetic modern language teachers in this country[1]. I cannot undertake to discuss here even the best books and pamphlets on these new methods. They will be enumerated in a special chapter, and students and teachers should make a point of reading the principal ones.

These lectures are especially intended to be suggestive, and, in my own small way, I hope to kindle your enthusiasm. Instead of discussing many different modern methods[2], I shall venture to lay before you my own opinions and experiences, together with my reasons for holding the former. I propose to throw out some hints on all the more important points of modern language teaching in schools, and shall take my instances mainly, but not exclusively, from German. On the whole it may be taken that what holds good for German holds good for French, but one important fact should never be lost sight of, viz. that the children beginning German in our schools are, as a rule, considerably older than those beginning French. If French is the first or, at the most, the second foreign language learned, German is usually either the third or the fourth, and is as a rule only taken up in the higher forms of boys' schools. For this reason the necessary elementary drill cannot be provided by means of the same kind of exercises that will do for very young children. The beginners in German invariably require a better mental pabulum—a fact that has often been overlooked. It is also very unwise to start German immediately, i.e. only one or two terms, after French—one

[1] Their views, experiences and suggestions are recorded in the volumes of *The Modern Language Quarterly* and *Modern Language Teaching*.

[2] See Miss Mary Brebner's pamphlet 'The Method of Teaching Modern Languages in Germany' (London, 1898), Chapter v.

language should be allowed to have a fair start before another
is begun.

I suppose I may take it for granted that you are all more
or less well acquainted with the general methods of teaching,
and have some notions as to what can be reasonably expected
from school children.   I can therefore restrict my observations
to the more technical part of the modern language teaching
in Secondary Schools and the various questions intimately
connected with it.

Some years ago there was a great deal of controversy as to
the educational value of modern languages[1]—fortunately that
time is now definitely past.   People are becoming more and
more anxious that modern languages should be taught, and
should be taught efficiently by thoroughly well trained teachers.
I firmly believe that there is a great chance for good modern
language teachers in the immediate future, that great opportunities will before long be given, and that all we have to do in
our schools and universities is to prepare ourselves most carefully
so as to be ready when the time comes[2].   It should not be said
of us 'Aber der grosse Moment findet ein kleines Geschlecht.'

The question arises: How should the necessary improvement in the teaching of modern foreign languages be effected?
I think it can be brought about if the following five conditions
are fulfilled :

(1)   More time should be allotted to the study of modern
languages at school.   This is of paramount importance.   Our
leading public schools should set the example[3].

[1] See, among others, C. Colbeck, 'On the Teaching of Modern Lan-
guages in Theory and Practice,' Lecture I. Cambridge, 1887, Fr. Storr,
'The Teaching of Modern Languages' (1897), p. 274, and H. W. Eve,
'The Teaching of Modern Languages' (1901, reprint 1905), pp. 230 sqq.

[2] See my pamphlet on 'Greek and its humanistic alternatives in the
Little-Go,' Cambridge, 1905.

[3] In fixing the times it should be borne in mind that for school-children
6 periods of 40 minutes are more helpful than 4 periods of an hour, and
4 periods of 45 minutes better than 3 periods of an hour.

(2) This time should be used much more systematically, with special reference to the educational needs of the pupils, and not merely with regard to the requirements of certain examinations. A great deal of harm is done to modern language teaching throughout the country by the conflicting regulations of our host of examinations—even though many of them have done a great deal of good in their time and may still have much to recommend them—and by the fact that many of them are still conducted exclusively by means of printed papers and without any compulsory oral test[1]. This seems to me a fatal mistake. The modern tongues should not be treated like the classical dead languages; a viva voce test should as far as possible be insisted on, in spite of the many practical difficulties of which I am well aware. Written examinations for beginners, especially by outside examiners who are not members of the school staff, should be discouraged.

(3) The classes in which modern languages are taught should be of a manageable size, and should, if possible, not exceed twenty to twenty-five pupils. They should be taught in special rooms, removed from the noise of the streets, and where the acoustic conditions are particularly favourable. Their decoration should, as far as possible, be characteristic of the foreign country. In large schools there should be at least one German and one French class-room containing large wall-maps of the foreign countries[2], photographs, pictures and picture post-cards of all kinds, portraits or busts of some of

---

[1] In the London University School Examinations an oral test is compulsory.

[2] Ed. Gaebler's school wall-map of Germany, 'Deutsches Reich, Niederlande, Belgien, Schweiz und deutsch-österreichische Länder, politisch. Bearbeitet und gezeichnet von Ed. Gaebler. Leipzig, Kartographische Verlagsanstalt von Georg Lange,' deserves to be strongly recommended. Other good political maps of Germany are 'Bamberg's Schulwandkarte' and 'Kiepert's Schulwandkarte.'

the great classical authors, collections of coins, flags, a phonograph, etc., and a well supplied library of suitable foreign books
and magazines.

(4) From the very beginning none but duly qualified
teachers should be entrusted with the teaching of modern
languages. The qualifications which I believe to be desirable
are discussed in a lecture first given in 1894 before the
College of Preceptors, and now reprinted, with some modifications and additions, on pp. 86 sqq. See the Report on
Training just published on behalf of a Select Committee of the
'Modern Language Association' in 'Modern Language Teaching.' I have been told that the qualifications desired in
my paper were too high for human capacity to attain, that
they represented the ideal rather than the feasible. My
answer is that I know from experience that in many cases the
ideal *has* been reached, that I believe that in another twenty-
five years it will be realised much more completely, that the
training of a modern language teacher does *not end* with his
having taken his University degree[1], and finally that it is a
mistake to put one's ideal too low. He who forms an educational or any other ideal must set it high ; time will show if he
was right or if his demands were excessive. I confidently leave
you to judge for yourselves.

(5) There should be a more general agreement as to the
chief points of method to be adopted and the books to be
read in school. To this fifth point I wish to devote special
attention. It is the one which is still engrossing the attention of
modern language teachers in this country[2] and abroad.

[1] See pages 107 sqq.

[2] See the valuable discussions in the *Journal of Education*, in the
School World, and especially in the *Modern Quarterly of Language and
Literature* (since 1897), and in *Modern Language Teaching* (since 1905)
which no serious English teacher of Modern Languages should leave
unread. Cp. also the Bibliographical Appendix, pp. 114 sqq.

Methods.

There are in the field many different methods of teaching modern languages—each claims to be the one true method,—all have zealous adherents—and I need hardly tell you that all promise wonderful results—most of them in a remarkably short time too[1]. Still it seems to me, and my experience as a teacher and examiner confirms my impression—that 'the true method' has not as yet been discovered.

It has not been discovered either in England or abroad.

I certainly do not flatter myself that I have discovered it. I doubt if one uniform method applicable in all cases—a universal panacea which nobody can modify with impunity—can ever be devised. I even doubt if this would be desirable. But it is clear that we are just now in a time of transition and experiment, and I think we have arrived at an agreement on several essential points. Many practical and experienced teachers in this country as well as abroad are at present actively working in this field; much that is good has of late been said and written on the subject,—and much, as it seems to me, that is quite worthless, unscientific and impracticable; a universal agreement even on all the principal points of method has not, however, as yet been arrived at. Much more interchange of ideas and experience is required. The chief work is still being done in Germany, Scandinavia, France, and America—England, in spite of a few noteworthy exceptions, has unfortunately till pretty recently lagged behind, but has during the last ten or twelve years made great progress.

Before going into details I should like to caution intending teachers on one or two points :

(1). Do not be *too* confident with regard to certain new methods, especially do not believe too easily in certain 'practical' ones which promise to teach many wonderful things

---

[1] See Canon Bell's paper, mentioned on page 118.

in a very short time.   These short cuts to proficiency are mostly
very unsatisfactory, containing one good idea, but carrying it too
far to the neglect of everything else.   They are as a rule more or
less mechanical, of but little scientific, literary, or educational
value ; they afford a certain routine, but do nothing to form and
educate the minds of the pupils.   They merely aim at drilling the
pupil in the use of a number of commonplace phrases and small
everyday chit-chat.   But the acquisition of a certain practical,
though naturally very limited, command of a modern tongue
by means of some series of words and phrases, the knowledge
possessed by head-waiters, couriers and interpreters, although
it is no doubt sometimes useful, cannot be the chief aim
of modern language teaching in our higher schools.   A
language which has so subtle and elaborate a syntax as
French, or a language which is so deeply saturated with poetry
as German, cannot and ought not to be studied by older boys
and girls after the unconscious fashion of an infant !

(2)   Again, method itself, even the best method, however
important, is not everything.   A very great deal of the
success depends on the natural gifts, the previous training,
the energy and the experience of the individual teacher[1].   It is
well known that the best modern language scholar does not
always obtain the best results as a teacher.   Consequently the
ideal modern language teacher will not only be a well-trained
scholar[2], but in addition something of an artist and of a man
of the world.   He must have the power of speech, an easy
mastery of the foreign idiom, and the gift of drawing out his
pupils and of making them speak, one and all, the shy ones
no less than the others, at every lesson.   He must have,—
more I think than any other master,—the great gift of readily
imparting his knowledge, of really interesting his pupils in using
the foreign idiom and in studying foreign life and thought,

---

[1] See *Modern Language Teaching*, II. 1 (February, 1906), pp. 14—15.
[2] See pages 93 sqq.

and of enabling them not only to *speak* but to *think* in the foreign language. I fully agree with the experienced pedagogue, Dr Münch, who at the general meeting of German modern language teachers held at Hamburg in 1896, insisted that "a teacher should have a certain amount of natural eloquence, quickness of perception, and appreciation of foreign character, as well as an interest in all that concerns modern life."

Whatever the method adopted may be, each master will vary it to some extent in accordance with his own individuality and the requirements of different sets of pupils. A good master will continually modify and improve his ways of teaching in the light of his extending study and increasing experience.

Nevertheless, although the possession of a certain, even of a very good, method is not all that is wanted by a young and zealous teacher in order to command success, it would not be right to underestimate its value. On the contrary, it is most important for us to make up our minds as to what seem to be the most satisfactory principles to be generally adopted in modern language teaching.

Happily on a few important points there seems to exist even at the present day an almost general agreement among experts. Let me take these first. They are:

(1) It is necessary that modern language teachers should have a much longer and better training[1] than they have had up to now in the great majority of cases. Their preparation should be at once more scientific and more practical. The improvement of the masters must needs precede the improvement of the children entrusted to their care. The number of

---

[1] On the *method of training of Modern Language teachers* see pp. 86—113; also cp. Bruno Busse, 'Wie studiert man Neuere Sprachen? Ein Ratgeber für alle, die sich dem Studium des Deutschen, Englischen und Französischen widmen,' Stuttgart, 1904 (with many bibliographical references). I am myself preparing a book on the study of German at British Universities.

hours modern language masters are expected to teach per week should be reduced to about 18, and should in no case exceed 20. Five hours per day is decidedly too much for any teacher who wishes to obtain good results and to keep in good health.

(2) Modern languages should *not* be taught in the same way as the ancient tongues. But even with regard to these there have been of late remarkable signs of improvement in books, texts, public utterances of leading scholars, etc. See, among others, W. H. S. Jones, 'The Teaching of Latin, London, 1905, and Dr Rouse's article on 'Translation' in the *Classical Review*, June, 1908, pp. 105—110. The modern languages are not studied mainly in our schools for the sake of their form, not even exclusively for the beauty and value of their literature, however important, but *in teaching modern languages we also aim at teaching in the broadest outline and as far as it is possible with young people the principal features of the life, character and thought of great foreign nations*. Modern languages should not only or mainly be studied and taught by means of translation-exercises, by getting up many paragraphs of grammar, remembering rare exceptions and turning over the pages of dictionaries. There should be no lessons more interesting and delightful to children than a modern language lesson given by the right teacher.

(3) And again, modern languages should be much more closely connected with the study of English on the one hand, and with History and Geography on the other. If groups of languages are studied together, those naturally related to each other should be taken by preference. French should be connected with Latin, and German with English. From a purely theoretical point of view it is even desirable that the two foreign tongues should not be taught by the same person, as not many men will possess the power of transforming themselves now into a Frenchman and now into a German with equal ease and success. There are, on the other hand, many advantages

in entrusting the teaching of English or of Modern European History and Geography, all of which are often sadly neglected at school, to a modern language master who is qualified to teach them. At present, however, most headmasters wish their modern language masters to be able to teach both German and French.

I have maintained that modern languages should *not* be taught in the same fashion as the ancient classical languages. Much greater stress must be laid on the language as a *living* and *spoken* organism. Hence it follows that

(*a*) *Pronunciation* should be most carefully taught by trained teachers and from the very first lesson. The pronunciation of the children should be correct from the beginning and should become easy and the intonation idiomatic through much practice. This aim can only rarely be reached by mere unconscious imitation ; a certain amount of phonetic drill is, in the case of some especially difficult sounds, absolutely necessary in order to shorten and to smooth the way of the pupil. No one should undertake to teach modern languages, especially to beginners, who has not previously had some training in the elements of phonetics.

(*b*) *Ordinary phrases and characteristic idioms* should be taught from the very beginning. The children should learn to choose them correctly and to use them readily. And lastly,

(*c*) Their *vocabulary* should be made as large and as useful as possible.

Under the old system of studying modern languages cases like the following often occurred : a great scholar would read French easily, but would scarcely understand a word of the spoken idiom if a French colleague happened to address him in French. Another scholar would write German fluently and without a single grammatical mistake, but it would be mere book-German, a dictionary language, a 'papierner Stil,' as it has been called by O. Schroeder[1], a language in which there

---

[1] Otto Schroeder, 'Vom papiernen Stil,' Leipzig, [6]1906.

would be scarcely a single sentence such as a German would write. A letter on ordinary topics `written by this scholar would smack so much of translation and be so utterly academic and unreal that it would require re-writing from beginning to end in order to become living German. On hearing a noise outside he would perhaps say: 'Welches ist doch jenes Geräusch, welches ich eben jetzt dort ausserhalb vernehme?' while a German would say: 'Was ist denn da draussen für ein Geräusch?', or possibly in familiar language: 'Was ist denn draussen los?' Only the other day I heard a gentleman who professed to know modern languages well say in a public lecture *home* for *homme*, *vou* for *vu*, and *Enfenk* for *Anfang*, *swonsig* for *zwanzig*, *Stŭdĭen* for *Stŭdĭen*, etc.

It is not easy to say to what extent oral and colloquial German and French should be combined in school teaching with the study and analysis of the written literary language. Different schools have different aims and needs. In order to arrive at a satisfactory conclusion and to strike a fair balance between the views of the old school who almost exclusively studied the written language of a few select classics, mostly poets, and the modern extremists who condemn whatever is not colloquial and, in their dread of elegant diction, often recommend and teach in school a familiar language bordering on slang, or a pronunciation such as *kek* for *quelque*, etc., it will not be out of place before going any further to investigate still more carefully and to settle definitely for ourselves the question: *What should be the aim of modern language teaching in our Secondary Schools?*

We cannot ask merely: What is desirable on general theoretical grounds? we are obliged to ask: What *can* be done in a *limited* number of lessons with *children*? Hence it seems to me that 'a practical mastery' of a foreign language, as promised by some methods, cannot possibly be hoped for. How many adults can confidently assert that they are absolute masters of their own language? But a good deal may be done at school, and whatever is learned should be learned well so as to awaken a life-long interest in the modern languages and the literatures written in them, and also to become a good basis for later practice.

What will be of paramount importance to most learners in after-life? Here I deliberately look for a moment at things from the utilitarian point of view and maintain the following propositions:

Not one of them will have to translate English works into foreign languages (we are of course not concerned with the training of interpreters and professional translators).

Some may be called upon to speak fluently in a foreign tongue.

Some may wish to translate from the foreign idiom into English.

Others may wish to correspond in the foreign tongue, but

All want to read foreign books, periodicals and newspapers, and to enjoy the treasures of foreign literature. All will one day be anxious to have some knowledge and to form a just appreciation of the general character, thoughts and manners of their neighbours and fellow-workers in the great field of European civilisation. For this most important aim their school teaching should fully equip them. Hence it follows that *reading, and not translating, should be placed in the foreground.* (On the use of translation see the debate of the Mod. Lang. Association, December 23, 1902, in *Mod. Lang. Quarterly*, 1903, and the papers published in Volumes III and IV of *Modern Language Teaching* (1907 and 1908), especially in Vol. IV. 2 (March, 1908).) 'Sprachgefühl' should be early aroused and carefully fostered by much reading of first-rate modern authors and by constant oral practice. A sufficient amount of grammar should be learned chiefly, although not exclusively, from the reading and a subsequent systematic analysis of the most important sentences[1]. But in school (the University system is of course

---

[1] See F. Spencer's ' Aims and Practice of Teaching' (Cambridge, 1897), pp. 100 sqq. and J. Findlay's ' Preparation for Instruction in English on a

different) grammar should not be taught for its own sake, but rather as an auxiliary subject, to promote the full and proper understanding, and to facilitate the reproduction or imitation, of the author's words and phrases. Translation from the foreign language into good and idiomatic English (not the usual shocking translation-English) should be practised only in cases of real difficulty, after the first foundation has been laid in class. At an *early* stage some very easy original composition in the foreign language, based throughout on the vocabulary and stock of idioms acquired at school, might be attempted with advantage. But *very* little ordinary composition, i.e. translation from English into the foreign language, should be done at first, and only with the more advanced pupils. Insistence on composition, however elementary, from beginners is, I believe, the greatest mistake made in our schools and by our examination authorities. The worship of early composition in French and German is as unjustifiable as it is detrimental to the best training in the lowest forms. In almost all schools composition is begun much too early, when the children know but little grammar, have met with hardly any idiomatic turns and phrases in their reading and class teaching, and have consequently not yet developed any 'Sprachgefühl.' Most examinations unfortunately still require a piece of unseen composition at a stage when the children cannot possibly be expected to produce a piece of decent composition of ordinary difficulty. The regulation requiring early composition and the pieces set for it may look very nice on the syllabus and in the printed papers of certain examinations—but read the Examiners' Reports in order to estimate the *value* of the work sent up by the vast majority of the junior candidates.

direct method' (Marburg, 1893). See also some of the pamphlets and essays enumerated in the Bibliographical Appendix, especially those by Max Walter, W. Rippmann and O. Siepmann, in which different views are ably advocated.

Rather set them some easy original composition or some kind of reproduction, and insist on their reaching a reasonable standard of proficiency, or give the pupils taught by more modern methods the option between ordinary and free composition, insisting in the same examination on a slightly higher standard of attainment in the case of the latter. Original compositions or reproductions are easier than translations from the mother-tongue, and are at first better calculated to make the children enter into the spirit of the foreign language. In saying this I do not mean that I should like to give up the valuable practice afforded by ordinary composition in middle and upper classes. For older boys and girls regular practice in translation from English into the foreign language seems to me to be absolutely indispensable by the side of free composition. The writing of easy letters on familiar subjects which would interest the children should be encouraged early and practised constantly. Little stories read or told by the teacher should be reproduced by the pupils, longer stories briefly recapitulated, short accounts of ordinary things and occurrences should be frequently given. The children should be encouraged to write and to speak about all they have actually seen and experienced. As far as possible during a modern language lesson no English appellation should stand between the objects and their foreign name. But in certain cases the giving of a brief English rendering may be by far the best thing to do, and in such cases the master should beware of making himself the slave of his general principle. In higher forms paraphrases of easy poems should be attempted, and at the end of their school time the most advanced pupils and candidates for scholarships might write about the principal characters in a story or a play which they have read, or on similar subjects. Some of the best pupils might also be induced to take part—under due supervision—in the lately instituted International Correspondence between pupils attending German, French and English schools. This movement is a recent one, but much good is reported of it[1].

Having now settled the various preliminary questions concerning the requirements and aims of modern language teaching, I shall proceed to the more detailed discussion of the teaching of pronunciation, spelling, grammar, and similar points of language, while in a subsequent lecture I shall discuss reading, composition and the study of reading-books, the proper selection and explanation of authors, and the teaching of the history of foreign literature. In a third lecture I shall speak of some special points referring to the teaching of German only. A final lecture will deal with the training of modern language teachers.

---

[1] Apply to Miss Lawrence, at the *Review of Reviews*, Mowbray House, Norfolk Street, Strand, W.C. and read her article in *Modern Language Teaching*, II. 3 (April, 1906), pp. 88 sqq. See Cloudesley Brereton, 'The Teaching of Mod. Languages,' London, 1905, p. 42. In 1904 a 'Société d'Échange International des enfants et des jeunes gens' was established, the founder and director of which is M. Toni-Mathieu, 36 Boulevard de Magenta, Paris. There is a similar undertaking by Mr Victor Willemin, Villa Monplaisir, Épinal (Vosges), France, concerning which all desirable information is given in the pamphlet (published by Prof. Willemin) 'Nos fils à l'étranger. Échange des jeunes gens et des enfants.' 1 Year's Report. Épinal, 1906. Of late the Modern Language Association has given attention to this question and a very fair measure of success has attended its efforts to promote the exchange of children during the holidays or for longer periods. Working in co-operation with the 'Société d'Échange International' at Paris, our Association has in 1908 arranged for some 35 holiday exchanges as against 23 in 1907, and for about 12 for longer periods. A list of 15 more French families who are seeking exchange for 6 or 12 months was received from Paris in Sept. 1908. Exchanges for Germany are still badly wanted, and it has been found more difficult to get these than exchanges for France. The only cost to parents, besides travelling expenses, is a fee (at present 5s.) to the Association. All communications on the subject should be addressed to Miss Batchelor, Grassendale, Southbourne-on-Sea, Hants. See also *Modern Language Teaching*, IV. 3 (April, 1908), 93 sqq., IV. 8 (December, 1908), 249—251, and Professor M. Hartmann's annual reports in *Die Neueren Sprachen*.

Pronunciation.

Any child that is instructed in a foreign language has a right to hear and to learn from his teacher a correct and idiomatic pronunciation of the foreign tongue. Am I wrong if I maintain that in many schools, even in good ones, this condition is at present far from being fulfilled? I do not require a teacher to dwell too long on phonetic niceties or to give a great deal of precious time to the teaching of phonetics pure and simple. There is neither time nor need for that [1]. He should at first speak and read to his pupils a good deal himself, in order to train their ear and to accustom them to the characteristic sounds and the peculiar intonation of the foreign idiom. His own intonation should be free from local or individual peculiarities, his enunciation should be clear and careful, but natural and free from affectation. After his pupils have been steeped, as it were, in the foreign element and have become somewhat familiar with the foreign way of articulating sounds, words and phrases, the master will make them repeat his sentences over and over again, immediately and carefully correcting mistakes of any importance. He will not infrequently make the whole class pronounce some sentences or even sing little poems *in chorus*, in order to force shy and backward pupils to speak out and to form their sounds after the model of the others. He will thus readily detect the faulty pronunciation of an individual child. The chief difficulties will be noted down and tabulated. Viëtor's *Lauttafeln* (for German, French, and English) or Rippmann's Sound Charts (English-French-German, published by Dent, 1*s*. net : small reproductions, 30 for 1*s*. net)

---

[1] I need hardly insist on the importance for the teacher of knowing something of English phonetics generally and in relation to German and French phonetics. For a first orientation nothing can be more helpful than a perusal of W. Rippmann's excellent little book called 'The Sounds of Spoken English,' a manual of ear training for English students. London, Dent, 1906, [2]1907. 1*s*. 6*d*. net.

should be used throughout in connection with this work. They should be hung up in the class-room. They will be continually worked at, every mistake pointed out on them, and thus the difficulties will finally be overcome by the large majority of children[1]. Such difficulties for instance are the French front vowels with lip rounding, and the nasal sounds, *cousin, mon oncle, on entre,* etc.; the *l mouillé* in *famille, feuille, Corneille, Versailles,* and the *n mouillé* in *agneau,* the guttural *r* in French and German, the pure (undiphthongised) long vowels and the modified vowels in German, the German initial *z,* the *ich* and *ach* sounds, the *ng,* etc. In French, the front rounded vowels, as in *pu, peu, peur,* are seldom properly acquired, no difference is made by many children between *vu* and *vous,* or *vu* is pronounced like *view, Victor Hugo* as *Victor Yoogo.* The instruction in actual phonetics should of course be as short and as simple as possible, but its fundamental physiological principles should be imparted even to children, and Bremer's Wandtafel 1 might well be hung up in the modern language class-room for occasional reference. Use might also be made of the book by Daniel Jones, '100 Poésies enfantines recueillies et mises en transcription phonétique. Illustrations par E. M. Pugh.' Leipzig, Teubner, 1907. The children should be told and shown that the spoken words consist of sounds and not of letters (e.g. *veau, deuil, feuille; champs, chants; schwarz, stehen, sprechen,* etc.). There is no very great difference in the pronunciation of the German *Vieh,* the English *fee* and the French *fi,* although the vowel sound is sometimes a diphthong in the English word (*=fee^{ee},* phonetically *fij* or *fi:i*), especially in Southern English. Again a teacher would probably seize an opportunity of showing the children that our ordinary alphabet is not by any means

---

[1] On the whole question see the able lecture ' On the use of Phonetics in Modern Language Teaching' by Dr Paul Passy, an abstract of which is printed in *The Modern Quarterly of Language and Literature,* 1 (1898), pp. 64 sqq.

complete, as it is far from representing each sound occurring in a language by a special symbol, but uses the same letter for various sounds, e.g. *ch* in *ich, ach*, or *b* in *Weib, Weibes, ng* in *der Ganges* (river) and *des Ganges* (walk), *e* in *wer, werden* (three kinds of *e* !), *o* in *doch, hoch*, or in *Schoß* and *schoß*; or *a* in *hat, man, father, small, care*, or *oo* in *good, floor, flood*; or *th* in *thin* and *thine*; *g* in *gin* and *gun*; *l* in *fusil, péril* and *fils* ('sons' and 'threads'); *ll* in *famille, ville*; or *g* in *gant, mangeant*; or on the other hand, different letters may represent the same sound, as in *Sie, sieh*; *Mal, Mahl, Maal*; *wir, ihr, vier*; *war, wahr*; *Haar, Schar*; *bot, Boot, droht*; *ältern, Eltern*, etc. Again—and here lies a great source of danger with regard to idiomatic pronunciation—the same letter may represent more or less different sounds in different languages, and in pronouncing foreign words the child should be early accustomed to give to the letters their foreign and not their usual English pronunciation, e.g. 𝔐𝔞𝔫𝔫 and *man*, 𝔥𝔞𝔱 and *hat*. In the case of the German words the mouth is in this case much more opened and the vowel sound perfectly short. The German *Quell* 'source' is to be pronounced *kvel* (bilabial or labio-dental, but without protruding the lips at all), the English *quell* is *kꭒell* with a strong protrusion of the lips. Or again, in many German words the characteristic 'glottal stop' or 'glottal catch' should be carefully noticed, e.g. *Verein* (= *fər'ʔain*), *erörtern* (= *ʔər'ʔərtərn*), *abändern* (*'ʔapʔɛndərn*), *entarten* (= *ʔənt'ʔa:rtən*), *geachtet* (= *gə'ʔaxtət*), *Wachtelei* (= *'vaxtəlʔai*), *Entenei* (= *'ʔɛntənʔai*), *Glückauf* (= *glyk'ʔauf*), and compare *verteilen* (= *fər'tailən*) and *enteilen* (= *ʔənt'ʔailən*); *entern* (*'ʔɛntərn*) and *enterben* (*ʔənt'ʔɛrbən*); *erröten* (*ʔə'rø:tən*) and *eröffnen* (*ʔər'ʔøfnən*); *Quälerei* (*kvɛ:lə'rai*) and *Adlerei* (*'ʔa:dlərʔai*); *Wüstenei* (*vy:stə'nai*) and *Straussenai* (*'ʃtrausənʔai*); *Vogelei* (*fo:gəlʔai*) and *Lorelei* (*'lo:rəlai*), etc. The 'glottal stop' is formed by bringing the vocal chords together, so as for a moment to close the glottis, and then suddenly opening them with an explosion, as is done, more violently, in coughing,

or in clearing the throat.   It is not a sound difficult to produce[1],
but, as it is not specially indicated in German writing and
printing, it is often neglected by English teachers of German.
It explains the German practice of breaking up words—which
differs from the English—thus *ge-ben*, and not *geb-en*.   Students
who wish to speak German at all well must be careful not to
neglect the glottal stop, and must make a clear distinction in the
pronunciation of words such as *vereisen (=fər'ʔaizən)* and *verreisen*
(*fə'raizən*), and also make a short break in *der eine, der andere,
zur Änderung*, and so forth.   See Miss Laura Soames, 'Introduction to Phonetics,' p. 146, W. Viëtor in 'German Pronunciation,' pp. 56 sqq., W. Rippmann, 'Elements of Phonetics,' pp.
6, 24, and my word lists in Series I and II of the 'Cambridge
Phonographic Records,' German Series, Records 95 and 107.
(Apply to Mrs Frazer, St Keyne's, Grange Road, Cambridge.)
The not unfrequent change of accent in the same word in the
case of many ordinary foreign words and the different quantity
and quality of their final vowels should be carefully pointed out
and practised, e.g. *Professor (pro'fɛsɔr), Professoren(pro·fɛ'so:rən)*;
Charakter (ka'raktər), Charaktere (ka·rak'tɛ:rə), etc.

   A word exists as a rule only as part of a phrase, hence the
proper reading of whole sentences should be started at once.
Here the characteristic foreign intonation and the peculiar
accent of the phrase should be carefully taught from the
beginning.   The teacher should insist on his pupils reading
and reciting the French sentences in the even, rhythmical
and distinct manner which is so characteristic of the French
enunciation.   He should not allow them to jerk out the words
one by one as is so often heard in oral examinations, but should
strictly insist on their emitting them in breath groups, producing
one continuous flow to the end of the sentence or part of a
longer sentence, however slow the pronunciation of the whole

---

[1] It is sometimes heard in emphatic English speech. See W. Rippmann,
'The Sounds of Spoken English,' p. 12.

group of words may be at first. This is often neglected in
school teaching, the masters being too easily satisfied with a
fairly correct pronunciation of individual words. Reciting
should be regularly and carefully practised from the beginning,
and here, as well as in teaching the pronunciation of separate
words, a good phonograph or gramophone will be found of
great value. The mechanical uniformity of the instrument
enables pupils to learn a piece of poetry or a song far more
quickly than if it were recited or sung to them by the master,
who, however good, is certain to vary slightly his articulation
or expression with each repetition, and so confuse and distract
the children's minds. There are now very fair instruments obtainable at a reasonable price, and it is not too much to hope
that before long the instruments may be still further improved.
Dictation also is of great value in training the ear to catch foreign
sounds quickly and reproduce them correctly, and is far too much
neglected in many schools, especially in the large public schools
for boys. In order to ensure success it is essential that both
teachers and pupils should have a good pronunciation, otherwise confusion between such words as *vous* and *vu, feu, fut, fou,
désert* and *dessert; Ähre* and *Ehre, Schiffe* and *Schiffer, Goethe* and
Götter, Gase and *Gasse, gesogen* and *gezogen, Saum* and *Zaum,
Hölle* and *Höhle, wagt* and *wacht* will inevitably occur.

In order to teach pronunciation effectively, most advocates
of the 'Neuere Richtung' strongly recommend beginning with
an easy phonetic transcription of foreign texts and not letting
the children see the ordinary spelling at all during the first few
weeks (or months). They maintain that children will catch the
foreign accent very much better if they do not start with the
confusing spelling of the present day, and they are of opinion
that the transition to the ordinary spelling later on is not nearly
so difficult as one would believe. They say that the experiment has frequently been tried with excellent success, while
those who most strenuously oppose it have never given it a
fair trial. This vexed question (of which I have no practical

experience) is still much discussed and far from being settled[1].
Practical experiments by competent, well-trained teachers are
still welcome, but it seems to me that the number of advocates
for beginning with phonetic script (at least for French) is on the
increase. Skilful teachers have no doubt obtained good results
from it, as I know for instance in the case of the boys taught
by L. von Glehn at the Cambridge Perse School for Boys.
Still, as far as I can see at present and have been able to
gather from the experience of others, it is not absolutely
necessary to introduce transcribed texts—indispensable as no
doubt they are for students and teachers—into class teaching.
Dr Passy's system (elaborated in 1888) as used in his periodical
'Le maître phonétique,' and introduced into many English,
German and French primers of modern languages, bids fair to
become the recognised International alphabet for phonetic
transcriptions. Teachers should read his 'Exposé des principes
de l'Association Phonétique internationale,' 1905, which may be
obtained for 6*d*. from Dr Passy, at 20 Rue de la Madelaine,
Bourg-la-Reine, Seine, France. This pamphlet also contains
a useful list of the principal works on phonetics and specimens
of phonetic transcriptions in the different European languages.
The 'Association Phonétique' was founded in France in 1886.
Single words of exceptional difficulty might at all events be
transcribed in class teaching in the symbols of this alphabet.
The books on phonetics from which a teacher will derive
useful information are enumerated in my 'Handy Guide,'
§ 4, b, and in Dr Passy's pamphlet 'Aims and Principles of
the International Phonetic Association,' Bourg-la-Reine, 1904.
I can specially recommend Viëtor's 'Kleine Phonetik des

[1] See *The Mod. Quarterly of Language and Literature*, II. 150—3 and
157—8; the Interim Report of the Mod. Lang. Association Sub-committee
on Phonetics appeared in the *Modern Language Quarterly* of April, 1899,
pp. 318—321. Mr D. L. Savory, in his Introduction to Calvert's and
Hartog's 'First Book of French Oral Teaching' (London, Rivingtons,
1906), has given strong arguments in favour of phonetic notation.

Deutschen, Englischen und Französischen,' Leipzig, 1897, together with the useful translation and adaptation of it by Walter Rippmann (London, ⁴1907), and also W. Rippmann's recent little book on the 'Sounds of Spoken English,' London, ²1907, Henry Sweet's book 'The Sounds of English, an introduction to phonetics,' Oxford, 1908, 2s. 6d., and D. Jones, 'The Pronunciation of English,' Cambridge, 1909. Otto Jespersen's 'Lehrbuch der Phonetik,' Leipzig, 1904 (adapted from his Danish 'Fonetik,' 1897–9), goes more into details and will be especially useful to more advanced students of phonetics[1].

After the ordinary pronunciation has been thoroughly mastered by the children, the teacher should discuss with them, as occasion arises, noteworthy exceptions occurring chiefly in the rimes of the classical poets. The apparent irregularities of French rimes such as *roi : parlerais : François* should be explained by an account of the earlier pronunciation of *-oi* (like *oè*). The rimes of Schiller and Goethe, e.g. *glühn : ziehn ; erzeigen : erzeugen ; Euch : bleich ; drei : treu ; Vergnügen : Griechen ; Zeichen : Zeugen ; kröne : Träne ; erbötig : gnädig; Chören : lehren ; an : Bahn ; keck : weg ; Getose : Schoße ; Schoße : Rose ;* etc. are not impure in the South German dialectic pronunciation of these great poets. In the highest forms an occasional word about the *changes* of pronunciation and the *standard* of pronunciation would not be out of place.

---

[1] For French pronunciation, Léopold Sudre's 'Petit manuel de prononciation française à l'usage des étrangers,' Paris, Didier, 1903, Benjamin Dumville's 'Elements of French Pronunciation and Diction,' London, 1904, and Karl Quiehl's 'Französische Aussprache und Sprachfertigkeit, ein Hilfsbuch zur Einführung in die Phonetik und Methodik des Französischen,' 4th revised Edition, Marburg, 1906 (bound, 5s. 6d.), deserve to be warmly recommended. See also E. Braunholtz, 'Books of Reference for Students and Teachers of French,' London, 1901, where useful lists are given on pp. 32 sqq. and 45 sqq. For German pronunciation see pp. 66—75, 93—4, 97—9, 140--2 of this book.

Spelling.

As to *Spelling* a word or two must suffice. German spelling
will be discussed in a later lecture. In nearly every language
there is a discrepancy, more or less marked, between the way
in which the words are written and that in which they are
pronounced. The spelling is not so arbitrary as is often
supposed, but represents an earlier stage of pronunciation : it is
more or less 'historic' (cp. *knight, veau, Stahl*). Much has
now simply to be committed to memory, but again the advantage of a good pronunciation on the part of the children will
clearly show itself. If children have been taught from the
beginning to distinguish in French properly between *e, é* and *è*,
they will without fail write *réponse*, but *repos*, and *représenter*,
père, and *désespéré*, and they would not write : '*deux cents
pierres* de Rome' instead of '*de Saint Pierre* de Rome.' If
they are accustomed to pronounce the German modified
vowels—one of the greatest stumbling-blocks in the way of
English students of German—no confusion between *Tochter*
and *Töchter, Burgen* and *Bürgen, gewahren* and *gewähren* ;
Drucker and *Drücker* ; *Buhne* and *Bühne* ; *geachtet* and *geächtet,
tauschen* and *täuschen* ; *Kampfer, Kämpfer* ; *Madchen, Mädchen* ;
schatzen, schätzen ; *zahlen, zählen* ; *dorren, dörren* ; *stutzen,
stützen*, etc. would be possible, and they would write : *der
Wind rauscht in den Blättern* and not *in den Blattern, es klingt
mir in den Ohren* and not *in den Öhren, was sagst du da?* and
not *was sägst du da?* They would distinguish in writing
between *Hüne* and *Hühner*, between *reisend, reissend* and
reizend, between *Senne, Sehne, Szene*, and *Zähne*. It is acknow-
ledged on all hands that the best way to teach spelling is
frequent dictation. Consequently writing from dictation should
in the earlier stages be part of the regular drill. In many
schools dictation exercises are unduly neglected in junior forms,
and bad habits are allowed to grow up which it is sometimes
very hard to eradicate. The proper way of dividing words

(which is not the same in English and in German) and also punctuation (e.g. the German habit of invariably putting a comma before *daß* and before relatives) should receive due attention; the use of semicolons, colons, inverted commas, and marks of interrogation and exclamation is often sadly neglected by children when writing down a dialogue from dictation.

Grammar[1].

It is pretty generally admitted that hitherto the getting up of grammatical niceties and curiosities has been far too prominent in most of our schools, and that Grammar should not be taught and learned at school principally for its own sake—not even in our modern 'grammar schools.' It should be taught in order to explain difficult passages and in order to

[1] I will here only touch in passing on a question that has recently begun to attract much attention, viz. should the mother-tongue continue to be used in teaching foreign grammar, and should grammars written in English still be put into the hands of children learning French and German? I believe that the time has not yet come to pronounce definitely on this point—so much depends on individual circumstances of teachers and pupils that the laying down of a general rule seems out of the question.

One thing, however, cannot be doubted. French grammars used in France by French children, and German grammars written for German children, ought *not* to be introduced into our schools. In every case the special difficulties of English-speaking children ought to be treated at some length, while niceties, interesting to foreigners, but comparatively unimportant to English children, should be strictly eliminated. If this is skilfully done, and French and German grammars—or rather the essentials of French and German grammar—are written in French and German for English-speaking pupils, they may probably be put to excellent use in the higher stages. A few French grammars of this description (by Berthon—Poole—Hartog—and Anderson) are now available, but—as far as I am aware—not yet a German school grammar written in German. In the lower stages, however, where every word of the foreign language proves difficult for the young beginners, and explanations cannot be too simple and easy, I very much doubt the advisability of starting with grammars or editions with introductions and notes written in the foreign language. The little time that at most schools is available for modern languages may be spent more profitably on texts of greater interest.

help the pupils to group together, to compare, and thus better to understand certain important linguistic phenomena. The study of grammar and the careful analytical examination of sentences are no doubt a most valuable mental training— although it is wrong to say, as is often rashly done, that the study of grammar is a study of logic; grammar is often *not* logical—still the special and minute study of grammar as such is not school work, but should be left to the scientific treatment of the University. Every school child should know the chief points of the ordinary grammar of the foreign tongue—he might even be shown how to make his own grammar (see page 78); but only the master should have made it a special study. *He* should of course be thoroughly well grounded in his grammar; moreover—and this is important—he should be able to give, wherever it may be desirable, the 'why' no less than the 'what.' He should know the historical or phonetic reasons of the chief grammatical phenomena[1]—but it would be a grave mistake if he were to introduce much of this special knowledge into his class teaching. The classics should be read and enjoyed— I am not sure whether they always are at present—and they should certainly not be turned in class into a hunting-ground for grammatical curiosities. The somewhat elaborate notes to the classics in the Pitt Press and similar editions are merely intended to facilitate home preparation, and to help the pupils thoroughly to understand the words of the text; they are certainly not meant to be learned by heart in order to be reproduced in examination papers. They are intended to relieve the teacher and to give him time for the reading aloud of the text with proper pronunciation and intonation, and also to facilitate a short and stimulating discussion of the scenes and characters of great plays, for which it is so often urged there is no time left in class teaching.

[1] See pp. 82—3, and also Ernst Laas, 'Der deutsche Unterricht auf höheren Lehranstalten' (2nd ed. (by J. Imelmann), Berlin, 1886), pp. 217—222.

From this there follows as the very first precept addressed to the teacher of foreign grammar : Do not burden the memory of your pupils with too many rules, still less with numerous lists of words following their own rules, those words which we call 'exceptions,' and which are generally so very largely utilized by a vast number of examiners whom I wish I could call exceptions also. All that we want to teach and to impress firmly on the memory of the children is a number of ever-recurring facts; certain rules, briefly and clearly expressed, and as far as possible deduced from the texts by the children themselves; and in addition to these only a very few of the most noteworthy exceptions. Most 'practical school grammars' contain far too much; they would certainly be twice as good if they were half as full[1]. They should chiefly be used by more advanced pupils as books of reference.

Another important point is that the rules should invariably be *preceded* by a number of well-chosen instances, selected phrases from which the pupils with the assistance of the teacher will find it easy and interesting to deduce the rules for themselves. This is the natural process of thinking—by comparison of similar facts the underlying law is discovered[2]. All the rules which a teacher wants to impress upon his pupils, he should as far as possible make them find for themselves. The process may be at first somewhat slow, but the interest of the children will never be allowed to flag, and ultimately the rules will be much better known, being remembered in their application and not merely in themselves. Nothing should be given to learn that has not first been carefully explained in class.

Our model teacher will, I fear, in many cases have to make up his own illustrative sentences, for what shall we say

[1] The well-known 'Skeleton Grammars' by H. G. Atkins (London, Blackie) certainly serve a very good purpose in the earlier stages.

[2] This point is not by any means 'new,' but was emphasized by Comenius ('Janua Linguarum Reserata,' 1631) and others.

of ready-made exercises such as the following : Decline in full :
'The blind mouse,' or of the exercise on the numerals : 'Have
you got two apples?' 'No, but my four sisters have six
dolls'?...I have often pitied teachers and pupils who had to
work through elaborate grammars, often containing subtle
distinctions of which the Germans themselves are entirely
ignorant and which only live an artificial life in the German of
certain examination papers, such, for instance, as that capital
distinction between *der* Vorwand and *die* Vorwand, of which
the latter is hardly ever—if at all—used in ordinary German
speech.   You might read in connection with this a pamphlet
which, although it is full of exaggerations and indeed not free
from mistakes, yet contains a great deal of truth ; it is 'The
caricature of German in English Schools,' by C. A. Musgrave,
London, 1894, and also G. G. Coulton in 'Public Schools and
the Public Needs,' London, 1901, in which a shrewd observer
has given facts about modern language examinations that afford
ample food for reflection.

Must, then, grammar be dry and repulsive to children ?   It
certainly was so under the old system when all schools were
'grammar schools' in the strictest sense of the word.   But
cannot even Dame Grammatica be made attractive to the
minds of the young?   I think she *can*, and I have no doubt
that everything depends on the way in which a teacher introduces her to the children.

First of all he will not give too much at a time, and that
modicum chiefly in connection with the passages read.   He
will also give the children some idea as to the actual meaning
of 'rules' and 'exceptions,' and keep the rules, i.e. the large
groups of facts, constantly before them, so as gradually to
develop their *Sprachgefühl*, that unconscious and unerring
feeling for what is idiomatic and right, the creation of which is
one of the highest aims of the teacher.   He will discuss the
terms 'regular' and 'irregular' in the proper way and choose a
few easy and striking instances for his explanations.   Even chil-

dren at school should sometimes get a glimpse of the ' why ' and the ' how,' although often they have of course only to remember the very commonest ' what.' With children of the *highest* forms even a few somewhat more advanced grammatical phenomena may be discussed as occasion offers itself, viz. the problems of ordinary form-association (i.e. the line in Goethe's ' Legende vom Hufeisen': *Das ein zerbrochen Hufeisen was—was*, now *war*, through form-association with the plural *waren*; but cp. English *was* and *were*, where the old difference is preserved); the development of Latin words in French, German and English; the two large groups of words which are distinguished as 'mots populaires' and 'mots savants' (*meuble, mobile—Kerker, Karzer—sure, secure*), the former being the older group in which the words have undergone the effect of the usual sound-laws of the language. Of course *all* such instruction should be kept *strictly* elementary—yet it would be sure to interest the children and give them more correct notions of the growth and development of language. The linguistic relation of English to French and German should be briefly and clearly explained. The relation of numerous words such as *finir* and *finish*, or *Leib* and *life*, might very well be shown. (Classified lists of correspondences between German and English words are given in my edition of ' Doctor Wespe' by R. Benedix. Pitt Press Series, 1888, ² 1895.) Rather than not touch at all on these and similar points, sacrifice the greater number of exceptions, in fact a good deal of what is given by our 'practical' grammars in small print, which should not be 'got up,' but only referred to as occasion offers. The brief explanation of some important general phenomena is of far greater educational value than a somewhat mechanical drill in rare exceptions or seldom used words and phrases—a drill which is really quite beside the mark in school teaching, and can no longer be half excused by pointing to the requirements of certain school examinations. Most of these have of late undergone very considerable alterations in the right direction.

Idioms.

The study of idiomatic phrases and the acquisition of a useful vocabulary cannot be begun too early. But only the really current idioms should be committed to memory, all slang should be carefully avoided, and sentences, not isolated words, should be learned. The principal idioms should be imparted gradually and, where this can easily be done, explained. Ancient manners and bygone customs have left many an interesting trace in the idiomatic phrases of everyday speech. An explanation of German idioms such as *einem die Stange halten— einen im Stiche lassen—mir schwant Böses—einem ein X für ein U machen—einen Korb bekommen—in die Schanze schlagen—auf die lange Bank schieben—den Kürzeren ziehen—kurz angebunden sein—etwas ausbaden müssen—einem das Bad heizen* or *segnen, einem die Brücke treten—einem die Leviten lesen—einem einen langen Salm machen—Stein und Bein schwören—einem den Daumen aufs Auge setzen—etwas bei einem auf dem Kerbholz haben—viel Geschrei und wenig Wolle—sein Schäfchen ins Trockne bringen—einem das Handwerk legen—einem den roten Hahn aufs Dach setzen,* and many others, would not fail to arouse the interest of the pupils and set their imagination going ; it would give occasionally some information about old German life and customs, and thus help them to remember the idioms which in most schools are unduly neglected. The necessary books of reference for the teacher of German are given on pp. 142—3 and in my 'Guide' on p. 39 ; teachers will find Borchardt(-Wustmann) especially helpful. There are some smaller books intended for the use of the pupils, e.g. those by Koop (London, ²1891), Becker (London, 1891), and Weisse (London, 1892), Taker and Roget (London, 1900), but all have certain shortcomings, and a really first-rate book of selected idioms for class purposes has still to be written. For French there is the useful book on ' French Idioms and Proverbs,' compiled by de V. Payen-Payne (London, ⁴1905).

Vocabulary[1].

Apart from the vocabulary, which the pupils will gradually acquire in a somewhat haphazard way from the reading of foreign authors, the teacher should from the beginning aim at adding systematically to the stock of words learned by his class. He will do this by regular discussions of small groups of words which are either connected by their sense or by their form and which, after they have been explained, will be learnt by the class All the ordinary incidents of everyday school life, the technical terms of question and answer, getting up, coming to the blackboard, opening of books, etc., may very well be discussed by the teacher almost from the beginning in the foreign language. The pamphlet by Holzer and Schmidt (see p. 120) will help the English teacher with regard to French, and a German counterpart could easily be devised. He will at first form short sentences showing the ordinary use of these words, or, in lower forms, have recourse to pictures composed for the purpose (e.g. Hölzel's well-known ' Wandbilder für den Anschauungs- und Sprachunterricht,' 14 pictures, Wien, Hölzel[2]), or the many useful ' Tableaux auxiliaires Delmas ' (16 pictures) avec livret explicatif par E. Rochelle, chez Delmas, Bordeaux *or*

[1] See also W. Rippmann in *Mod. Lang. Teaching*, IV (1908), 236—244.

[2] In connection with these may be used the booklets called ' Konversations-Unterricht nach Hölzel's Bildertafeln' (German, French, Italian, English) published by Emil Roth at Giessen. The German, French, etc. parts can be had separately. And cp. now M. Walter, ' Aneignung und Verarbeitung des Wortschatzes im neusprachlichen Unterricht,' Marburg, 1907 (München lecture of June, 1906, enlarged), and also Kehr's ' Der Anschauungsunterricht für Haus und Schule,' Gotha...Perthes (quoted by Walter in his ' Aneignung etc.' p. 15) ; or the ' Description des tableaux d'enseignement d'Ed. Hoelzel à l'usage des écoles' par Lucien Génin et Joseph Schamanek, Vienna, 1905 (1s. 3d.). The First French Book and the First German Book in Dent's series will also be found most useful in this respect. In their latest editions there are many improvements, not the least among them being (in the French book) the new pictures of the seasons with French—instead of Austrian—local colour.

London, Hachette and Co., or to W. Rippmann's French and German Picture Vocabularies (London, Dent, since 1906, two series in French and in German, price 1*s*. each.)   He will take such series of words as: father, mother, child, son, daughter...i.e. all those expressing ordinary family relationships. Another day he will take: house, court, garden, street, road;... or sun, moon, star, cloud, thunder, lightning...the sun sets, a cloud covers the moon, the thunder roars, the lightning flashes, the rain falls *or* pours down...; or tree, bush, oak, beech, fir, willow...together with the verbs; to plant, to grow, to burst into leaf, etc.   The teacher will do well to work the necessary words and phrases into short and interesting dialogues, or into stories which he will tell the children several times in the foreign language and which he will make them repeat, write down from dictation, and learn by heart.   Irregular verbs should at first be avoided as far as is possible.   Subjects such as 'a walk in the country,' 'a birthday party at home,' 'a school-treat,' 'a thunderstorm at sea,' 'a cycling accident in the street,' 'a visit to our uncle at Berlin or Paris,' would afford plenty of useful material for increasing the vocabulary of the pupils. The numerals, the pronouns, and the forms of address make natural groups which should be studied together and worked into a number of well-devised sentences, and letterwriting— addresses, beginnings, endings—should be taught at school, a few models of each being given.   Together with the numerals the chief foreign measures, weights and moneys should be given with their English equivalents.   Some foreign coins should be shown to the class when their name and value are given.   The Educational Supply Association now sell a set of German coins (facsimile) for 4*d*. which should form part of a collection of modern language 'Realia' at every school. Coloured picture post-cards (1*d*. each) giving splendid reproductions of foreign coins used also to be obtainable but are unfortunately now out of print.

Another way of systematically increasing the vocabulary,

which is often very useful with more advanced pupils, is the study of ordinary words which are connected by form : *sitzen, setzen, Sitzung, Satzung, Sitz, Satz (Aufsatz, Einsatz, Vorsatz, Absatz), Setzer, besitzen, aufsitzen, absitzen, nachsitzen, einsetzen, absetzen, versetzen, übersetzen, besetzen, Besitzung, Besatzung, Besetzung, Versetzung, Übersetzung,...*or *steigen, Steig (Bahnsteig, Steigeisen, Steigbügel), Stieg (Aufstieg, Abstieg), Steg, Stegreif, ab-, auf-, aus-, ein-, um-steigen...*etc. The difficulty here is where to stop, but the conscientious teacher who has prepared his lesson beforehand, and has made for himself a carefully considered list of the words which he intends to give his pupils, will not be exposed to the danger of giving too much, viz. words which are of but little practical importance for school purposes. Word-formation is at present far too much neglected in school-teaching.

A third way of systematically widening the vocabulary, and one which should only be used occasionally in the highest forms by a skilful and well-informed teacher, is the method (so far as it can be used) of etymological comparison. The lists of ordinary sound-correspondences in my Pitt Press edition of Benedix' comedy 'Doctor Wespe,' with numerous instances for every sound compared, will be found useful for this purpose. No doubt the pupils in the higher forms will be interested in occasional comparisons of words the meaning of which is now widely different, but where the German explains the English, or where the English throws some light on the German word, e.g. *glatt—glad* in *Gladstone, satt—sad*, or (*Steinhuder*) *Meer—(Winder)mere*, etc. See p. 101.

With regard to systematically imparting to the class a good working vocabulary I should not advise teachers to confine themselves to one of these methods only—some change is always refreshing—but to take the first-mentioned method as a foundation, and to make the children learn, gradually and systematically, *all* the most important words of the foreign language—and none but those.

Some hints how this may be done are contained in a German pamphlet on the first teaching of French. It is by Dr Hermann Soltmann, and is called 'Das propädeutische Halbjahr des französischen Unterrichts an der höheren Mädchenschule,' Bremen, 1893. Further hints may be obtained from 'Das Vokabellernen im französischen Anfangsunterricht,' by G. Wendt, Leipzig, 1901. What is said there with regard to French at German schools holds equally good with regard to our English schools. Short but useful guides for English teachers of French and German have recently been written by W. Rippmann ('Hints on teaching French,' London, 1898, ⁵1906; 'Hints on teaching German,' London, 1899, third edition, re-written, London, 1906), who has also contributed some valuable articles on the early teaching of French to the first numbers of 'The School World' (1899). On the first teaching of German see the excellent advice given by E. L. Milner-Barry in 'The School World' (Oct.—Dec. 1899).

Conversation[1].

It is of the utmost importance that a master should *talk to his class in the foreign language* as early as possible. He will begin by discussing pictures and objects which are placed before the pupils (e.g. Delmas', Rippmann's, or Hölzel's pictures; see above). For this he will find useful the 'Konversationsunterricht nach Hölzels Bildertafeln,' Giessen, Roth, 10 parts, each 40 pf. (i.e. 5*d*.), and 'Description des tableaux d'enseignement d'Ed. Hoelzel à l'usage des écoles par Lucien Génin et Joseph Schamanek,' Vienna, 1*s*. 3*d*. I have already mentioned E. Rochelle's 'Livret explicatif des Tableaux Auxiliaires Delmas,' Bordeaux, 1903. (Obtainable in London, at Messrs

---

[1] See the discussions in *Modern Language Teaching*, I (1905), Nos. 6 and foll., and the summing up in *M. L. T.* II (1906), pp. 11—15.

Hachette and Co., for 8½*d*.) At first, in order to be understood, he will occasionally have to give some short explanations in English, and he will not talk French or German the whole time. Gradually the necessary explanations in the English language will become less frequent and the talk in the foreign language will be continued longer. The master must from the beginning make all the children take an active part in the lesson, and consequently the modern language classes ought never to be very large. The pupils must be interested—stimulated to make out what the master says and to express in the foreign tongue what they see him doing. In spite of all his attempts to draw them out many of the boys will at first prove most determined 'passive resisters.' But the teacher must be equally determined not to give in. He will first train their ear and their faculty of catching the peculiarity of the foreign sounds and intonation, then their faculty of speech. He must make them answer in complete sentences—all of them, not only the few forward pupils—he must in every way endeavour to overcome their shyness and disinclination to use the foreign idiom. Most English school-boys are unwilling to try to speak any other language than their own, they think it affectation to produce a proper French nasal sound, and it will require all the skill and tact of a master in whom they believe to draw them out. He will naturally make them speak at first exclusively of things which they see or have observed and experienced, about topics well known to them, the vocabulary of which they have mastered. In order to do this the teacher must of course be full of resource, besides being able to converse in the foreign idiom with ease and fluency. A French candidate for the degree of Agrégé is required by the regulations of the examination to discourse for an hour in the foreign language and is then questioned on his lecture. A German modern language master is required in his 'Staatsexamen' to show fluency and correctness in the practical use of the foreign language which he wants to teach. Our English examination tests are in this respect as yet far from sufficient.   A change for the better seems however to be setting in[1].

In speaking the foreign language the teacher should with junior classes at first make use of some picture such as (the improved) Hölzel's, Rippmann's, or Delmas'. With older pupils who have done at least one other foreign language, a teacher of German may also take the map of Europe, and teach according to the direct method, beginning perhaps by pointing to England and saying[2]:

Dies ist England.   Was ist dies?   Dies ist England.
Dies ist Deutschland. Was ist dies? Dies ist Deutschland.
England (Deutschland) ist ein Land.   Das Land ist groß,
    das große Land.   Deutschland ist ein großes Land.
Dies ist die Nordsee.   Die Nordsee ist ein Meer.
Dies ist der Rhein.   Der Rhein ist ein Fluß.
Der Fluß fließt in das Meer (in die Nordsee).
Dies ist die Elbe.   Die Elbe ist auch ein Fluß.
Die Elbe fließt auch in die Nordsee.
Der Rhein und die Elbe sind Flüsse.
Die Elbe ist ein großer deutscher Fluß.

[1] At Cambridge a viva voce Examination on a much larger basis and of a much more searching nature than the old oral test has now been established for the Tripos, and oral examinations are also in existence at all the other leading Universities. For the latest German regulations see the *Ordnung für die Prüfung, die praktische Ausbildung und die Anstellung der Kandidaten des höheren Lehramts in Preußen*, Halle a. S., 1906, pages 7—8 ; 15—17 ; 85 sqq. See also pages 165 sqq. of this book.

[2] Cp. the excellent chapter on the teaching of German on a direct system by Fred. Spencer in his 'Aims and Practice of Teaching' (Cambridge, 1897), pp. 100—120. My specimen above given was constructed before the appearance of Mr Spencer's valuable experiment. On a similar experiment (by Mr Findlay, Mr Twentyman and Mr Kirkman) see the Bibliographical Appendix p. 119, under 21 and 32. In both cases the pupils were adults. But I cannot see any strong reason against starting with foreign life and ways in the case of young pupils. The mental difficulties will not be insuperable, the interest will be much quickened by the charm of novelty and the pleasure in comparison.

A number of questions and answers—carefully pronounced —would serve to make the children familiar with the foregoing sentences and the sounds contained in them. Then a summary of the grammatical material contained in these sentences would be made by the teacher, speaking English, thus:

Der, die, das—ein—dies—groß; großer, große, großes— ist, sind—fließt—Fluß, Flüsse—der Fluß, das Land, das Meer, der Rhein, die Elbe, die Nordsee—England, Deutschland, deutscher—ein deutscher Fluß, ein großes Land.

It is scarcely necessary to remark that in the case of young beginners this would be far too much grammatical material for a single lesson. For a class of older boys and girls it will just be possible to master it.

Or a teacher might start with Rippmann's picture-books and discuss the scenes of everyday life with his pupils, especially with young children in the lower forms. With older children historical and geographical pictures, with which every school should be well supplied, should be discussed also[1]. In conjunction with these the teacher might use E. Lavisse's book of 'Récits et entretiens familiers sur l'histoire de France' (Paris, A. Colin). It is recommended by M. Walter in 'Die Aneignung und Verarbeitung des Wortschatzes,' pp. 17 ff., where a master of method has shown the uses to which these récits may be put.

In order to secure, without risk of losing it again, an easy command of the foreign idiom, teachers of modern languages should, after the completion of their University training, have

[1] During the last few years, as is well known, the Universities of Cambridge and Oxford have added to their Local and Joint Board Examinations voluntary oral tests in modern languages. It is to be hoped that the number of schools going in for them will rapidly increase. So far there are not many candidates, especially among the boys, and the results are often not yet satisfactory, but at all events a beginning has been made that is bound to develop. I have been assured that some excellent results are obtained at the London University School Examinations, where an oral test is compulsory.

resided abroad and should from time to time go abroad again.
But a prolonged stay in a foreign country will be valuable in
other ways also.   It will enable teachers to see with their own
eyes and to speak from personal experience.   They will be
more just and sympathetic in their judgment of foreign excellencies, foreign peculiarities, and foreign difficulties.   With
regard to the right interpretation of foreign life and thought to
the rising generation of their own country their task is one of
the noblest and of the most responsible.   It is to be desired
that modern language teachers in Great Britain and abroad
should always be conscious of their great responsibility.
Residence abroad is so far nowhere compulsory, no European
State requires it expressly of its modern language teachers ; but
in France, where of late the State has done much for modern
languages, to have resided abroad is virtually a condition of
appointment to good posts.   Travelling exhibitions are given
in Germany, Austria, Switzerland, and France by the State and
by municipalities ; and in Sweden, I am informed, on such a
scale that every modern language teacher has on an average, one
year in five at his disposal.   America gives a prolonged leave
of absence every seventh year, and also bursaries.   At the
Neuphilologentag at Hamburg (1896) it was resolved to
memorialise the German governments to the effect that 'for
the maintenance of conversational facility and the knowledge
of foreign life and customs, leave of absence should be granted
to teachers of modern languages—whether in Universities or
High Schools—at certain fixed intervals of time (at least every
five years),' and this was emphasized again at Cologne in 1904.
In England the State does not directly interfere, though it has
helped, in these matters, but it is very desirable that teachers
of modern languages should themselves help to keep up their
practical efficiency, and that headmasters should assist them
by granting an occasional leave of absence.   This is a point of
very great importance and one that the Modern Language
Association should be interested in taking up.   When he was

at Birmingham, Professor Fiedler succeeded more than once in raising a sum of £50 to be given as a travelling scholarship to students of the University. There have also been awarded at the Birmingham University the valuable Harding Scholarships for honours students of German[1]. With regard to subsidising duly qualified actual or intending modern language teachers, mention should also be made of the excellent facilities afforded by the Gilchrist Scholarships (given to Manchester, Liverpool and Leeds Universities) for honours graduates in modern languages; also of the West Riding scheme of continuing their Modern Language Scholarships for a 4th or 5th year for residence abroad. The London County Council has also repeatedly given travelling bursaries to modern language teachers. Thus a beginning has been made, but it is to be hoped that before long County Councils all over England and also private donors will do much more.

Very much good may be done by the new system of exchange of teachers, by which English men and women teachers are appointed as 'assistants' in French and Prussian state schools. Information on the conditions of this important scheme of 'assistants' in French and Prussian schools can be obtained by writing to the Director of Special Enquiries, Board of Education Library, St Stephen's House, Cannon Row, London, S.W.[2] It is essential that only modern language

[1] The regulations concerning the Harding Scholarships in German were (in 1907) as follows: A Scholarship of the annual value of £50, tenable during three years by students of German in the School of Modern Languages, may be awarded by the Faculty of Arts on the nomination of the Professor of German.

At the close of the third year a further Travelling Scholarship of £100 for one year may be awarded to the scholars, provided that he or she has taken the M.A. degree in the School of Modern Languages and that his or her work and conduct for the previous three years have been satisfactory. The Travelling Scholarship will be tenable at a German University, to be approved by the Faculty of Arts.

[2] See also pp. 85 sqq. of the *Ordnung für die Prüfung* etc., and pp. 170—1 of this book.

honours graduates, that is, only such men and women as have
made the study of modern languages their life's work, shall
ultimately be sent abroad by the Board of Education, and it is
moreover highly desirable that these 'assistants' should as far
as possible be attached to schools in foreign University towns.
They would thus enjoy, in addition to the opportunities offered
by residence in any foreign town, the many peculiar advantages
arising out of the facilities for study and research that can only
be found in academic surroundings.   See p. 118, under 12.

   At present there exist in a large number of French, Swiss, and
German University towns so-called 'Holiday courses' in which
lectures in the language of the country are given, opportunities
for the constant use of the foreign language offered, practice in
phonetic drill arranged, and illustrations in the methods of
modern language teaching given.   Such summer meetings are
being held in July and August at many German Universities,
for instance at Greifswald (on the Baltic Sea), Marburg (on
the Lahn), and Jena (near Weimar and the Wartburg).   The
French meetings are arranged at Paris by the Alliance Française
(apply to the Secretary, 45, Rue de Grenelle) and (at Honfleur,
Tours, and at Neuwied) by the Modern Language Holiday
Courses Committee of the Teachers' Guild (apply to the Secretary of the Teachers' Guild, 74, Gower Street, London, W.C.).
On the French and Swiss meetings see P. Shaw Jeffrey,
'The Study of Colloquial and Literary French,' London,
1899, pp. 35 sqq.   The Edinburgh Holiday Courses in which
much attention is paid to systematic drill in the use of modern
languages, especially of French, deserve to be recommended.
Many of my own students have derived the greatest benefit from
attending such courses abroad.   Moreover the *Ferienkurse* are
cheap, part of them specially devised for the needs of foreigners[1]

---

[1] The Holiday Courses held (since 1904) by the University of London
under the able directorship of Professor Walter Rippmann are only intended
for foreign students and teachers.   At the University Extension Meetings
held alternately at the Universities of Cambridge (1910, 1912, etc.) and

and, from all I have heard of them from a number of students
of both sexes, most enjoyable[1]. I have no doubt that our
students and teachers of modern languages will very largely
benefit by repeated visits abroad in the congenial society of
fellow-teachers, and in daily practice of the foreign idiom.
They should live, if possible, in a German or French family
where they could be the *only foreigners* (*not* merely the only
English boarders) and on no account go to one of the large
boarding-houses[2], which are obviously the most unsuitable
places to live in if one wants to learn a foreign language.

There is a growing conviction that the teaching of modern
languages in our secondary schools should henceforth, as
a rule, not be entrusted to foreigners, but to duly qualified
English men and women. I believe that this is a very sound
and well justified view—I cannot discuss it here at length[3]—and
the only advice I have to give to intending teachers, no less
than to those who have entered the profession, is : Go abroad
as much as you can, improve and deepen your knowledge of the
language and of the people as much as is in your power[4].

Oxford (1909, 1911) special attention is now also paid to the needs of
foreign students. The courses held during the month of August at the
University of Edinburgh are intended for British students of French and
German and for foreign students of English. Much good work is being
done at these courses under the guidance of distinguished professors and
skilled teachers, and they have proved useful to Britons and foreigners alike.

[1] See the *Journal of Education*, 1899, p. 151. A useful table of Holiday
Courses on the Continent for instruction in Modern Languages is now
annually compiled by the Board of Education. It is usually ready for
publication about the end of March or the beginning of April in each year,
and copies can be obtained from Messrs Wyman and Sons, Ltd., Fetter
Lane, E.C.

[2] This remark does *not* apply to Dr Schweitzer's 'Institut Français
pour Étrangers.' See p. 110.

[3] See my paper on 'The Teaching of Modern Languages' contributed to
Mr Spenser Wilkinson's 'The Nation's Need,' London, 1903, pp. 219 sqq.

[4] Books such as R. Kron's 'French Daily Life,' London, Dent, [4]1905,
Kron's 'German Daily Life,' London, [4]1905, and A. Hamann's 'Echo der

Here at Cambridge we have now (1908) for twenty-four years past been training teachers of modern languages, and there have been among them very few indeed who did not manage to go abroad at least once, during the three or four years they were reading for their Modern Languages Tripos[1]. Most of them went abroad two or three times during their residence. In order to derive real benefit from their stay abroad, students should not go too early and should very carefully prepare themselves for it. See also pages 109—112.

Reading.

As the object of modern language teaching is in my opinion to teach not only the foreign language, but at the same time, by means of it, the principal features of the life and character of a foreign nation, it follows that the material for reading should be chosen so as to promote this aim.

A most careful *selection* of suitable material should be made, and a systematic *gradation* of reading should be devised.

After a good many *object lessons* in which the common objects of the foreign country are called by their foreign names

deutschen Umgangssprache,' will be found most useful. Students should be provided with Jäschke's little pocket dictionaries of French and German, with the Baedekers of Paris (or Northern France, in French) or Berlin (or Norddeutschland, etc. in German); if they read German, students of French might consult Langenscheidt's 'Sachwörterbuch,' 'Land und Leute in Frankreich,' Berlin, [3]1905 (where other references are given); Mahrenholtz, 'Frankreich' (Leipzig, 1897); and Klöpper's 'Französisches Real-Lexikon.'

[1] An account of the history of the Cambridge Medieval and Modern Languages Tripos has been given by me in the April number (1899) of the *Modern Quarterly*, pp. 322—6. See also my account contributed to P. Shaw Jeffrey's 'Study of Colloquial and Literary French,' London, 1899, pp. 173—183. For the great changes introduced in 1907 by means of which the attraction of the Tripos has been largely enhanced, see 'The Student's Handbook to the University and Colleges of Cambridge,' Cambridge University Press, 1908, 3*s*., pages 348—364.

and discussed in a variety of sentences, there might follow the use of a *Primer* containing all the commonest words and well chosen characteristic illustrations. From the very beginning the reading should be connected with the history and geography of the foreign country. A good clear school-map of Germany[1] (or France) with German (or French) names should be hung up among other things characteristic of the foreign country, of its literature, institutions and principal buildings, in the German (or French) class-room. German names of German places, rivers (with the defin. article) and mountains should be taught throughout, e.g. Aachen, Köln, Braunschweig, Mainz, Regensburg, München, Frankfurt, Leipzig, Hannover, Wien, Donau, Weichsel, Vogesen, Pfalz, Thüringen, Sachsen, Schlesien, etc.

In the *middle* classes a well compiled *Reader* should form the centre of all modern language teaching. It would be a graduated continuation of the Primer used in the lower forms. The ideal German Reader for English Schools has not yet been written. E. Hausknecht's 'The English Student,' J. Klapperich's 'Englisches Lese- und Realienbuch,' perhaps also W. Viëtor's and F. Dörr's 'Englisches Lesebuch,' or O. Jespersen's and Chr. Sarauw's 'Engelsk Begynderbog' and O. Jespersen's 'England and America Reader' are the books which I should set up as models to be followed, but some of the pieces should even at this stage be chosen, without regard for practical utility, merely for the sake of their literary excellence.

In the *upper* forms the Reader should be replaced by the study of some of the best classical works, and to aid teachers in their choice of these, a select list or 'canon' of such classical works as are suitable for the pupils to read either in school or at home should be compiled by a committee of practical teachers[2], and a small library, containing a selection of suitable

[1] See page 5 note.

[2] See 'Französischer Lektüre-Kanon,' 'Verzeichnis aller bis zum 31 März 1908 vom Kanon-Ausschuss des Allgemeinen Deutschen Neuphilologen-Verbandes für brauchbar erklärten Schulausgaben französischer Schrift-

books in modern languages, should be formed for the upper and middle forms of secondary schools for boys and girls.

Nature of the proposed 'Reader.'

Our model 'Reader' for middle classes[1]—which is as yet unwritten—should contain only pieces illustrating the life and thought of the foreign nation in olden and, still more, in our own times. The selection should be made by an experienced teacher with skill and tact, and above all in a spirit of sympathy with foreign excellencies and of interest in foreign peculiarities. Its aim must obviously be to make the children understand foreign ways of thinking, but not to encourage in them a spirit of immature and self-assertive criticism. The texts should as far as possible be accompanied by well executed characteristic *illustrations*, showing for instance the Roland of Bremen, die Wartburg, or the Mont St Michel, or Notre Dame de Paris. A glossary at the end, with easy phonetic transcriptions of especially difficult words and proper names, and short references to obvious etymological comparisons with English, would much enhance the usefulness of such a Reader.

Anything not in harmony with these principles should be strictly excluded from the modern language reading books. From a model Reader of French or German I should, for instance, unhesitatingly exclude a description, however brilliant, of the 'battle of Marathon,' or 'a trip to the Isle of Wight,' or 'a sunset in the desert,' or 'the character of the Chinese,' or 'Warren Hastings.' I should also discard general anecdotes, such as 'remarkable cleverness of a fox-terrier,' or fables, such

steller, zusammengestellt von Dr W. Tappert.' Marburg, Elwert, 1908. 6d. Also 'Englischer Lektüre Kanon'...von Dr Curt Reichel. Marburg, Elwert, 1908. 6d. (Also up to 31/iii 1908.) Both reprinted from Vol. XVI of 'Die Neueren Sprachen.'

[1] For English students and teachers Wilh. Paszkowski's excellent 'Lesebuch zur Einführung in die Kenntnis Deutschlands und seines geistigen Lebens,' Berlin, 1904, ⁴1909, deserves warm recommendation.

as 'the boy and the serpent,' etc. On the other hand I should gladly admit 'a trip from London to Paris,' 'a visit to the South of France,' or 'to the Rhine,' or 'to the Black Forest,' a 'visit to the Louvre,' or 'to the Castle at Heidelberg,' or 'to Cologne Cathedral,' 'a reception into the Académie Française,' 'a Provençal vintage,' 'a speech by Bismarck in the Reichstag,' 'a German school-treat,' 'a Turnfahrt,' 'a Sängerfest,' etc. Again place might be found for subjects such as 'Henry IV and the foreign ambassadors,' 'the Emperor Max and his fool Kunz von Rosen,' 'Frederick II and the miller of Sanssouci,' 'Bismarck and the Austrian Ambassador,' or 'Goethe's correspondence with Carlyle,' or some letters of Lessing or Schiller or of Moltke or Bismarck.

In the case of German, pieces such as these would be just as useful to the pupils learning the language as those contained in the present books, and they would—each of them—in addition illustrate some point of German history, geography, life and thought, and would furnish excellent material for comparison and discussion.

In addition to the selected pieces in prose and verse I should put into the Reader:

(1) Good clear maps, not too small, of Germany and France; rivers and places to be given with their foreign names, the rivers with the definite article, *le* Rhône, *la* Seine; *der* Neckar, *die* Weser, etc. Special maps of Berlin and Vienna (or Paris) with their surroundings should be included.

(2) Tables of foreign measures, weights, and moneys (the latter if possible with coloured illustrations—few English children realize the size and value of a German Pfennig, an Austrian Heller, or have seen German nickel money), together with their English equivalents.

(3) Pictures of the flags and ensigns of foreign nations, also the German spread-eagle (as seen on all official documents), the emblem of the French Republic, and similar illustrations of importance and interest which can easily be procured.

(4)   Enumerations of the different social grades and their respective titles, together with the proper forms of address, and also the shape and style of gentlemen's and ladies' visiting cards.

(5)   Letters of various kinds, both ordinary letters (social and commercial) and some of a higher and of the highest type. Some of the German letters should be in German handwriting. Forms of envelopes with all kinds of addresses and directions, e.g. *Eingeschrieben, Postlagernd, Bitte nachzuschicken, Abs(ender)*, etc., and headings of postal wrappers (*Drucksache, Geschäftspapiere, Muster ohne Wert*, etc.), should also be given.

(6)   A few typical forms of advertisements, together with the useful notices of births, engagements (in Germany), marriages, and deaths.

(7)   A list of the most common abbreviations used in the foreign languages, such as the German *G.m.b.H.*; *a.D.*; *bezw.*; *Hss.*; *m.E.*; *s.Z.*; *D^r phil.*; *Dr Ing.*; *s.v.w.*; *u.ä.*; *ult.*, etc.[1]

A Reader containing all these items could most profitably be made the basis of instruction in the foreign tongues.

Study of the Classics.

For the use of the highest forms of schools a characteristic selection of truly representative works should be made, beginning with some rather easy works.   A sort of 'canon' of all that is really first-rate, and at the same time suitable for school-reading, should be drawn up.   This again would be a really useful subject for discussion among the members of the Modern Language Association, and the columns of *Modern Language Teaching* would be at the disposal of persons of experience anxious to discuss this most important problem. As but little time can be allotted to modern languages in the curricula of our secondary schools, it is of paramount importance that no book but the very best, the most suitable and the most

[1] Lists explaining all the ordinary German and English abbreviations are given in my revised edition of Cassell's German Dictionary (1906).

characteristic, should be set for school-reading or suggested for the private reading of the scholars. This is at present very frequently not the case; a number of the books prescribed and edited with English notes do not deserve to be studied in schools to the neglect of other works, which are no more difficult and far more attractive and important.

The 'canon' of works to be read should be sufficiently comprehensive to admit of frequent changes: at one time one of Lessing's plays, at another one by Goethe or Schiller or Grillparzer or some other great dramatist might be set, the same standard of difficulty being kept. But nothing that is not of real literary excellence should be read, and for this reason for instance Kotzebue's old-fashioned and one-sided farce, 'Die deutschen Kleinstädter,' which is at present much read in France and of which there is, unfortunately, also an English edition, should be sternly rejected. School-children would get nothing but wrong notions about German life from the reading of this farce, while a more modern and infinitely superior play, Gustav Freytag's comedy, 'Die Journalisten,' is not read half as much as it deserves to be.

In the lists of suitable texts, to be drawn up by the joint efforts of a number of experienced teachers, there should be columns for easy, intermediate, and difficult texts, subdivided into prose and poetry, with indications as to whether the texts are specially suitable for boys or for girls, or are well adapted for both sexes. Symbols might be added to show if the books are recommended for class-reading or will do for private study, and in every case the names of the editor and the publisher, and also the price, should be given. Such lists, which would have to be revised from time to time, would prove of great value to teachers and examining bodies[1].

A 'canon' of poems to be learned by heart—after due explanation and recitation by the master—should also be used.

---

[1] See Tappert's and Reichel's Lists mentioned on page 44 note.

There should be a gradation from the easier to the harder, and the older poems should be repeated from time to time in later terms [1].

Some prose pieces (fables, passages from speeches) might also occasionally be committed to memory and recited with suitable intonation by the class. If properly treated this is really a most useful exercise, but the master must take care that the piece is well explained, understood, learned, and recited without a hitch and with the proper intonation and expression. The pieces thus learned should be models of style and need not be at all long. Here is a large field for really useful investigation and much wanted reform. These exercises will be found to 'pay' all the better when our Modern Language examinations are still further reformed and due importance is attached to proficiency in the spoken language.

I sincerely trust that before long all the progressive schools in this country will assign more time to the study of modern languages, this being the first and foremost condition of success in teaching them. In the meantime

(1) Find out the number of hours per term and year at your disposal in your school; then

(2) Make a general plan of work on a clearly conceived system for yourself and your colleagues at the same school.

(3) Bring about a fruitful interchange of ideas with your fellow-teachers, as to what should be read and in what way you are going to read it in the different forms of the school.

The study of foreign classics in the highest forms [2] should be less dependent than it is now upon 'set books' appointed for examinations. The drawbacks of getting up 'set books' are

---

[1] During the first year of German some of the interesting and easy poems might be learned by junior pupils. The little book by W. P. Chalmers, 'Deutsche Gedichte zum Auswendiglernen' (with notes in either German or English), London, Harrap, [2]1906, 1s. 6d., will be found useful.

[2] In the lower and middle forms easy modern authors should be read by preference.

well known. They may be too hard or they may be too easy for a great number of pupils. They are often merely learned by rote—completely spoiling the child's pleasure in the book— and at all events a disproportionate amount of time is given in most schools to the getting up of one or two books, while four or five of the same size might have been read and enjoyed within the same space of time. Sometimes, of course, pre-scribed books may fit in well and be just *the* thing to study. But it cannot be denied that they often disturb the harmonious development of the subject, coming in at the wrong time for individual forms and taking the place of books which should be read by preference. The options that are now offered by some examining bodies are to be welcomed as a step in the right direction. The following is a true, though rather an extreme, case of the present neglect of the classics. Some time ago I had to examine orally a candidate who told me that he had done German for more than three years. When I asked him what authors he had read in this time, he answered, ' I have only read the set book, but I have worked through many—examination papers'! Others never read anything but extracts.

More than once I have been asked by teachers : Do you think that the French 17th and German 18th century classics should still be read in English schools? This question is most frequently asked by teachers who know only of utilitarian and commercial, but not of educational ends in the study of modern foreign literature. We should here beware of our friends. There is no doubt a decided increase in the interest taken in modern languages all over the country, especially in French, but this interest I am sorry to see is in many cases not educational but purely commercial. These advocates of ' Moderns versus Ancients' forget that education and culture are the ends of all higher school study, and that the very best is just good enough for the education of our children. That kind of education which the better schools should give cannot be got from the trashy stuff which some utilitarian pedagogues propose to substitute for the great works of the noblest minds. It is true that the study of Molière's *Misanthrope* does not always help us to read the advertisements of 'Le Petit Journal,' still less are Schiller's 'Wallenstein' or Grillparzer's 'Sappho' the most suitable preparation for the study of the 'Berliner Börsenkurier'—but I trust that you will all agree with me that, practical as the teaching of modern languages must be, teachers have no right to withhold from their more advanced pupils the knowledge of some of the greatest works of modern literary art, works full of beauty and of noble ideas expressed in exquisite language. It is the privilege of a teacher to show his scholars how these great works of art should be appreciated and enjoyed. His own zeal and enthusiasm should kindle those of his pupils. Above all, in schools in which the ancient classical writers are but little read or not read at all, all the more stress should be laid on the careful study of a number of foreign masterpieces of the 17th, 18th and 19th centuries. These convictions do not in the least prevent my admitting that some suitable and thoroughly modern texts should be read from time to time by the side of the great classics, especially in the case of an unusually short or crowded term. There will be ample time for reading a considerable amount of real literature on the modern sides of good boys' schools and in all the high schools for girls, as teachers in the future will devote less time to the teaching of grammar pure and simple, and very little to the mechanical manufacturing of colourless translations from English into the foreign language. Moreover private reading on the part of the pupils should be constantly encouraged and discreetly directed by the master, not only in the vacations when pupils of the higher forms might quite well be encouraged to read an interesting French or German book from the school or form library, but also during the school terms. As I have pointed out on page 5, every form, or at least each of the two main divisions (junior—senior), should have its special Modern Language Library—containing a good selection of fairly easy and well illustrated French and German books, some representative illustrated foreign magazines, some good picture books in the lower forms, some books on history and travel, and some good large maps (political as well as physical) of foreign countries with foreign names of rivers and towns, etc. The cost of providing such small libraries is not very considerable. Kind donors might like to help in starting them and their use would be very great. Boys and girls should be encouraged frequently to spend some of their leisure time with these books and, if their spare time is very limited during term, at least to look at the pictures and read what is said in connection with them. Much depends here, as in other cases, on the active interest shown by some of the members of the teaching staff in starting and developing such libraries, on their skill in obtaining donations and in securing the right sort of books. Many teachers are so far quite unaware of their opportunities in this direction, and they might profitably spend some hours abroad in acquainting themselves with the most suitable German and French books and pictures to be bought for their school libraries. See pp. 5—6.

The method of reading with a class[1].

The most careful preparation on the part of the teacher —and not only of the young teacher—is necessary for success. He has not merely to consider what is to be said, but what is not to be said, and, in the case of what he says, how best to say and impress it upon the minds of the young.

A good teacher will of course never be content with walking into his class-room and saying on the subject he is to teach just what happens to occur to him—he will carefully sift his material, reduce and simplify, dwell on the important points, in short, work according to a well-conceived plan and

[1] See W. Macpherson, ' Principles and method in the study of English literature.' Cambridge, University Press, 1908.

without omission of any point of importance for the children. The fact that everything has been thought out beforehand need not make his delivery dry and dull, either to himself or to his class. In order to make his lesson interesting and fruitful I would advise a young teacher as follows: Get from your class, as far as possible by means of question and answer, the facts which you have decided to teach. In coöperation with them extract everything that is of importance in the text you are studying, encouraging every child to help in the work. Be careful not to talk above the understanding of the children, especially of the average children, in the discussion of a great play or of a difficult poem—do not talk about what will interest *you* most, but about what the children want and have a right to learn. Great care and tact, also great self-abnegation, are necessary in the teaching of poetry and literature. The very best and deepest thoughts of the greatest minds are naturally beyond the reach of children—yet fortunately there remains a very great deal that *can* be taught, and, if imparted carefully and in an interesting manner, it will be sure to bear fruit in later life. The children should be early accustomed to look upon a poem or a play not as an exercise or as something to be crammed for an examination, but as a work of art to be appreciated and enjoyed. A good teacher will not use many words about it, but he will let this feeling arise naturally from the way in which he approaches and treats the poem. Before he begins to read a poem or a prose passage with the class he will be careful to create the proper atmosphere for it. A few introductory words will prepare the minds of the young, and then the poem will not fail to produce the desired effect upon them. But if you begin the reading of a poem by saying in a cold business-like tone: 'Smith, will you read the first stanza of poem No. 42 on page 96 of the Reader'—of course the Muse of Poetry will have left the room long before Smith has opened his mouth. All will be different if the teacher says a few simple words of introduction to prepare the minds of the children beforehand, and then proceeds to read the poem aloud with proper pronunciation, intonation and expression. Poems such as Goethe's 'Erlkönig' or Schiller's 'Graf von Habsburg' require very careful reading in order to produce the fullest effect. Few masters will be able to read these poems really well without careful preparation—perhaps with the assistance of a good phonographic record. After the master has read the poem he will have it repeated by the pupils, the better ones being first called upon, and will insist on a good, careful and spirited reproduction. Sometimes a short poem may be advantageously read by the whole class together. The teacher should explain any real difficulties and ask questions concerning passages which require explanation—but he should not create difficulties. In the case of poems it is sometimes advantageous to give and to require a prose rendering of difficult lines, or, before actually reading a difficult poem, to give the class a brief summary of its contents. Two poems which I have found to be hard to render well and which are not easily understood even by pupils of good ability are Schiller's 'Kampf mit dem Drachen' and still more Goethe's so-called 'Ballade' ('vom vertriebenen und zurückkehrenden Grafen'). Never give a poem to the class to be learned by heart without having first read and fully explained the whole of it. It is wrong to expect that this important work of initiating the children into a piece of foreign poetry should be done by the parents at home, or by the master supervising the 'preparation class.' The same remark applies to poems sung in class. Too often the children are allowed to sing French or German songs which they do not properly understand. Teachers should also avoid setting long poems in the lower and middle classes to be absorbed reluctantly in homœopathical doses during the whole of a long term by the unfortunate children.

With the highest forms you will be able to read pretty rapidly, making the pupils invariably read out the German or

French texts in a spirited manner and only requiring an English rendering or a German or French paraphrase in the case of rather difficult passages. If you attempt at *that* stage some of the great foreign dramas you will find that your pupils really enjoy them, not being obliged to take line by line and scene by scene like drops from a dropper—the safest way of making them detest Racine and Schiller for many years to come. Many mistakes are made by teachers in giving superfluous information or requiring the pupils to learn by rote all the notes contained in their editions of the classic. A great play is too good to be treated as a storehouse full of grammatical curiosities. These should certainly be explained in the notes where they occur, but their importance should not be exaggerated and no disproportionate amount of time should be allowed for them. In saying this I do not wish to recommend that the teacher should pass over unnoticed any real difficulty of language or thought, or should allow any opportunity for awakening literary taste to slip by.

In dealing with a great play, if it be written in verse, the teacher should consider it his duty briefly to discuss the *metrical* form, of which nearly all school-children and even many advanced students of modern languages are entirely ignorant. They should know the elements of poetic form—it is by no means a matter of no importance in what way the poet has chosen to express his thoughts. Certain forms suit the poetic genius of certain languages—the iambic trimeter is the national tragic metre for the Greeks, as is the alexandrine for the French, and blank verse for the English. Lessing and Schiller deliberately adopted in their later plays the English blank verse; Goethe's metre in 'Iphigenie' is more closely connected with the Italian *endecasillabo*; all three modified the adopted metre to suit their own taste and genius. Even school-boys and school-girls may fairly be expected to have some general notions on such points—which, if properly brought before them, would be sure to interest them: for instance, a word about poetical licence would not be out of place with a sixth form; the scholars should be warned against merely saying in the case of apparent or real metrical irregularities 'this is a poetical licence,' without having any clear notion of the precise meaning of this term. The use of vague terms should be discouraged from the beginning, and the characteristics of the few common dramatic metres should be familiar to every scholar who is allowed to read a great French or German classical drama. What is the state of things at present? Some years ago I had to examine a great number of schools in Schiller's 'Wilhelm Tell,' a play consisting of 3,290 lines. I ventured to ask the question: 'In what metre is this play written? Give a brief description of it.' Here are some of the answers which I read with a shudder I can still recall: 'This play is written in the old Italian ballad metre, that is, the metre of Virgil's Æneid,' or 'The metre of this play is called Alexandrine,' 'Schiller's Tell is written in didactic hexameters.' Such were the extraordinary statements to which they committed themselves after having read over 3,200 lines of blank verse! It was disheartening, and the worst was that children writing such absolute nonsense did actually pass the examination with credit if their grammar and translation were correct. Another time I was assured that Grillparzer's 'Sappho' was a 'trilogy,' because—there were three prominent characters in the drama (Sappho, Phaon, Melitta). Who was to blame? Not the children, but the teachers, who had plainly neglected to pay any attention whatsoever to form. A similar case is not unfrequent at a higher stage, where it often turns out that students coming up to the University cannot decently read a German hexameter—although they may have passed with distinction in their 'set book,' 'Hermann und Dorothea.' The elegiac metre of Schiller's grand 'Spaziergang' was actually called 'eccentric blank verse' by a candidate for a University Honours examination. Many intending modern language students coming up to the University are, up to the present, quite unable to give a definition of a 'pure rime' in German, or even of the principal difference between the dramatic verse of Schiller and Racine.

Another point at which the teacher ought to work with his class is the making clear to every child the general intention of the poet—the plot—the connection of the scenes—the main stages in the development of the action—the exposition, climax, peripeteia, and the catastrophe—in short what we may fitly call the 'inner form' of the drama, the moulding of the great mass of material in the mind of the poet so as to assume a higher artistic form.   Think of the masterly structure of Schiller's 'Wallenstein.'   Here the teacher can do very much to develop the taste, the judgment, and the general culture of his pupils. These lessons should be the finest fruit of all his teaching, they should never be forgotten.   How much can be done in this respect by the right man for a sixth form, I know from experience, gratefully recollecting a series of stimulating lessons on the German classics given during my last year at school by our headmaster Dr Wiedasch of Hannover.   But where is the corresponding teaching of English literature in many of our secondary schools?   No good work can possibly be achieved by a modern language teacher unless his pupils have first received a thoroughly good grounding in their mother-tongue. Great reforms in the teaching of English seem to me to be most urgently required in the immediate future in not a few schools[1].

If you read great plays with your best pupils—they should only be read with good pupils—sum up after each scene, after each act.   Discuss the development of the action, see how far it has advanced (and by what means), what is still expected (hoped or feared).   Discuss the characters and their motives, group them, see in what way they develop (if they develop at

[1] See 'The New Regulations of the Board of Education, on the Study of English in Secondary Schools,' printed in the *Educational Times*, Oct. 1, 1904, pp. 438—9.

all), and let some advanced pupils attempt to write very briefly in the foreign language about such of the characters as specially interest them. 'Goetz von Berlichingen,' 'Maria Stuart' and 'Wilhelm Tell' are easy plays in this respect; 'Minna von Barnhelm,' 'Iphigenie,' 'Tasso,' 'Die Jungfrau von Orleans,' and 'Wallenstein,' present greater difficulties[1].

A teacher is considerably helped in his task of explaining a play and the chief characters occurring in it, if he has seen it acted abroad by good actors. This is one among many reasons why teachers of foreign languages in going abroad should go to large towns, to great intellectual centres where there are good theatres. Paris, Berlin, Vienna and many large German towns such as München, Dresden, Frankfurt, Köln, Hannover, Hamburg, and many others, will in this respect supply all that can be desired. It is a great pity that there are still some students and teachers who are disinclined to go to the theatres—they certainly miss a great opportunity for the better understanding of the noble plays which they are called upon to explain to their pupils. It is a great mistake to ignore the obvious fact that plays are written to be seen on the stage and not to be read in an easy-chair. I cannot help feeling that he who allows 'moral' scruples to prevent his attending first-rate performances of the great modern masterpieces of dramatic art given by the best actors and actresses of our own times may be a most estimable person, but is wholly unsuitable for the office of teacher of modern languages. He would probably never care to do justice to Schiller's fine essay 'Die Schaubühne als moralische Anstalt betrachtet' and to numerous similar utterances by him, Lessing, Goethe, Grillparzer and Hebbel. A teacher of modern languages and literatures should do his best to cultivate and develop a taste for literary art for his own benefit no less than for that of his pupils. Teachers who wish

[1] Compare my article 'How to study a masterpiece of literature' in the *National Home Reading Union Magazine*, Special Course, October, 1895.

to succeed should be infinitely more than mere *maîtres de langue*. As to books for the proper explanation of German plays, those by G. Freytag, Bulthaupt, Bellermann, Franz, and others enumerated on pages 148—9, and in my *Handy Guide*, pp. 75 and 103, will be found useful.

One more remark before I leave this subject. If a play should happen to be historical, do not dwell on all the points in which a poet has purposely or unconsciously deviated from history, still less allow them to be crammed for examination purposes, but show, by one or two really striking instances, in what manner and for what reason a great writer of tragedy has treated and transformed the facts of history. Goethe's 'Egmont' and Schiller's 'Maria Stuart' or 'Jungfrau von Orleans' afford good examples. Again, if the play should happen to be Goethe's 'Iphigenie' (how many children pronounce the name of the heroine correctly?), do not waste much valuable time in pointing out conscientiously—if conscience has any part in such a proceeding—all the numerous cases in which Goethe differs from Euripides, but be careful to discuss fully the great difference of the spirit pervading the whole, the transformation of all the principal characters in Goethe's drama, and the all-important alteration of the ending.

The last question connected with modern language teaching with which I propose to deal here is

Should the History of Foreign Literature as such be taught in Schools?

I think not. It cannot and it should not. I do not speak of exceptional cases, as when boys or girls are reading for scholarships tenable at a University. It will be found difficult enough to give pupils in the highest forms some general notions concerning the development of their own national literature, a subject hitherto far too much neglected.

But a short biographical account and estimate of the position and literary importance of some of the most prominent modern authors—carefully prepared by the teacher and told in an attractive manner—may very well be given. The children should not only not be allowed to remain in complete ignorance of the authors whose works they are reading—a state of things that is unfortunately too common—but they should be told something about the greatest foreign writers, they should know the main facts of their lives, aims, and achievements—they should be shown pictures of them and be made to take a real interest in them. Wherever it is possible to do so, the chief characteristics of great foreign authors should be illustrated by short and well-considered comparisons with the greatest English classics[1]. But the foreign writers to be thus treated must only be the stars of the first magnitude. We must not attempt to do too many things in class teaching, but whatever we undertake to teach, let us teach well.

This is what I wished to say about the teaching of modern languages generally. I have an ideal before me of the manner in which a modern language teacher should set to work and of the success which he may reasonably hope for with children of ordinary ability and not extraordinary industry who get only a few hours of German and French a week, while all the other subjects are taught by means of the English language. Under ordinary conditions the pupils cannot possibly learn to swim freely in the foreign element, but they may and should take a great deal of interest in their work, lay a good and solid foundation at school, and—as the languages are modern and living—continue in later life to extend their knowledge of the foreign tongues and the great nations who speak them. The stimulus and taste for this study must be given in

[1] Cp. A. R. Hohlfeld, 'Der Litteraturbetrieb in der Schule, mit besonderer Rücksicht auf die gegenseitigen Beziehungen der englischen und der deutschen Litteratur,' an important lecture, printed in the American *Pädagogische Monatshefte*, Broadway, Milwaukee, Januar—Februar, 1902.

the first instance by their teachers—what a great and noble task is theirs if only they will approach it in the proper spirit! Even those whose interests are chiefly directed to the promotion of technical or commercial education and who realise the great importance of modern languages for these branches of human activity, should remember that all special training in technical and commercial subjects, if it is to be sound, must needs rest on a satisfactory basis of thorough general information. The teaching of modern languages, if properly promoted and improved, will no doubt produce much better results than it does now for the benefit of those who merely need these languages for technical or commercial pursuits—but the study and teaching of modern languages has a much higher aim and a much more important duty to fulfil in the curriculum of the secondary education of the twentieth century. At the beginning of our century I foresee a great future for modern language study in our schools—let us then all do our best to make the most of our great opportunities and never forget that, in spite of all the pressure from without, we must not degrade the study of modern languages to a successful analysis of the various types of business letters and newspaper articles, or an acquisition of a certain amount of everyday prattle on some trivial topics, but that it is our duty to teach modern languages in secondary schools as one of the most valuable elements in a truly liberal education[1].

[1] See Wilhelm Münch's valuable 'Ten Commandments for Modern Language Teachers,' propounded at the last Neuphilologentag at Hannover (June, 1908) and printed in *Die Neueren Sprachen*, XVI (August, 1908), 293, and also in the valuable *Bericht über die Verhandlungen der xiii Tagung des Allgemeinen Deutschen Neuphilologen-Verbandes zu Hannover vom 8. bis 12. Juni 1908*, Hannover, Carl Meyer (Gustav Prior), 1909, pp. 37—8. 3s.

THE TEACHING OF GERMAN IN OUR
SECONDARY SCHOOLS[1]

My aim is to throw out some hints as to the special objects
and the special difficulties of the teaching of German and to
give my opinion as to some much discussed points of spelling,
pronunciation, and reading, for it is of the greatest importance
that intending teachers should start with definite views on such
vexed points.   At present unfortunately the position of German
in most of the British schools—especially boys' schools—is
far from satisfactory.   This subject has of late been losing instead of gaining ground[2].   In most boys' schools it has never
yet had a fair chance, it has never been taken seriously—Clifton
College, Manchester Grammar School, and a few other schools
forming noteworthy exceptions.   This decline is due to circumstances over which the teachers have not had any control,
but it is a serious national danger which in the best interests
of higher education should be averted.   At all events the less
flourishing the general condition of the study, the better
equipped should the teachers of German be for their difficult
and responsible task.

Before entering into details I am anxious once more to say

[1] Readers of this chapter may like to work through the valuable
book by E. W. Bagster-Collins on 'The Teaching of German in Secondary
Schools,' New York, 1904.

[2] See 'Modern Language Teaching,' Vol. IV, 68–81; 118, 119; 133–5,
195—8.   A change for the better seems now at last to become possible.

most emphatically that to teach German in the highest sense, even in middle-class schools and to children of ordinary ability, does not merely mean to teach Grammar and Composition, or Conversation on a few everyday topics, but above all to teach the spirit of the language, the ready understanding and use of it, and by means of language and literature to spread a just understanding of the spirit of the German nation, and to produce a sympathetic appreciation of the life and thought of a people so nearly related to the English. The close connection of the two greatest Germanic peoples in language, literature and feeling should from time to time be pointed out. The interest in the study of a tongue so nearly akin to the English will thus be kept up and intensified[1].

On the other hand it will be the task of a good teacher to find out the chief and most characteristic differences between English and German. He will do well to note down all the main difficulties experienced by English children in learning German, to tabulate them for his own use, to keep them continually in view and to make the children pay special attention to them. By doing this he will bring it about that the chief and most annoying mistakes will disappear one by one, and that the children will leave school with as fair a knowledge of German as can be reasonably expected—a knowledge much superior to that now possessed by most pupils at school and by not a few students coming up to the Universities.

German Letters.

In a previous lecture I have discussed the relation of letters and sounds in a general way, reminding students of the

[1] English teachers of German may like to join the *Zweigverein London des Allgemeinen Deutschen Sprachvereins* (apply to the Secretary, Mr Max Sylge, 26—28, Sun Street, Finsbury Square, London, E.C.), or the *English Goethe Society* (apply to the Secretary, Dr Oswald, 29, Adelaide Road, London, N.W.).

facts that spoken words consist of sounds and not of letters, and also that the pronunciation changes more rapidly than the spelling, which on this account never accurately represents the actual pronunciation. To-day I have to deal with the German letters, the peculiar alphabet in use in Germany, Austria and Switzerland. The question arises : Should the use of German small and capital letters, written and printed, four new alphabets for English children, still be taught in our English schools? This is a question which is frequently asked. I have no hesitation in answering that they should certainly be taught from the beginning[1], the new letter in connection with the foreign sound[2]. The initial trouble is not very great, and the reason for incurring it is, that whatever the absolute or the scientific value of the German alphabet may be, yet as long as the great majority of Germans use the German letters exclusively, it would be very wrong in English teachers to withhold from their pupils familiarity with these characters and not to train them in their use while they are young and can easily acquire them. It may hamper some of them very considerably in later life—I know it from experience—if they cannot read or write German characters with ease and fluency. Books from which the reading of the German handwriting can be learned are not wanting, see p. 140[3]. Clerks, officers, secretaries, persons travelling abroad, let alone scholars, will one day be

---

[1] Professor Rippmann advocates the adoption of German printing and writing after the initial difficulties of German have been overcome by the pupils. Consequently his First German Book is printed in Latin characters and the Second German Book in German characters. Another practical teacher of much experience, Mr Otto Siepmann, of Clifton College, at the beginning of his *Public School German Primer* prints the same passages on the same page first in Latin and then in German characters.

[2] This is called in German *Schreiblesen*.

[3] For exercise books for writing German apply to Mr Nutt, 57—59, Long Acre, W.C. There is also a ' copy book,'—' Modern German Writing,' by John Dalziel Maclean, London, Simpkin, Marshall and Co. ; and Glasgow, I. N. Mackinlay, 1900, 6*d*.

glad to be able to read German writing and German print. Even those who in later life do not actually need to read or to write the German handwriting may like to be able to write the language as the Germans do—they will look upon it as an accomplishment. It is true that in 'Local' and other Examinations candidates are 'not required,' nor even encouraged, to use the German handwriting, but this does not mean that those who write German really well are forbidden to write it. The examiners have found by experience that in most cases up to now the handwriting of the candidates has been too bad for them to encourage its use in examinations. Writing against time does not tend to improve any handwriting, and many pupils seem only to be able to draw German words letter by letter in a medieval monkish handwriting, and cannot possibly hope to finish their task in time if they use German characters. Some teachers who agree that the German handwriting should be taught, prefer to introduce it after the initial difficulties of the language have been overcome by the pupils. Professor Rippmann, for instance, prefers the German sound chart at the beginning. This is a question which teachers of German will eventually settle from practical experience.

The same remarks apply with still greater force to the use of German characters (*Fraktur*) in German books printed in this country, especially in English school editions of German classics. I think we are at present bound to keep them, and that teachers are bound to teach them. As long as most German books and all the newspapers are printed in German type[1] we cannot afford to neglect it. Knowing the history of the so-called Gothic or black-letter type[2] in Germany and elsewhere, I am far from seeing in its use something specially German

[1] See Johannes Schlecht's article 'Eckschrift oder Rundschrift' in the *Zeitschrift für den deutschen Unterricht*, VII (1893), 471—5; and E. Stengel's article 'Fraktur oder Antiqua' in the fortnightly magazine *Fortschritt*, published at Kiel, Vol. II, 7 (April, 1908), 194 sqq.

[2] See G. Hempl, *German Orthography and Phonology*, Boston and London, 1897.

which it would be a patriotic duty for the Germans to retain. I even wish the German type were replaced by the common round type (*Antiqua*) which for many reasons deserves to be recommended—still we teachers of German in England have no right to initiate so great a change and to deny to our pupils that proper training in the use of the German letters which cannot anywhere be given with more facility and success than at school. Why do we not first abolish the use of Greek and Hebrew letters in the grammar schools? They are certainly at least as hard—or not more easy—and not more practically useful to most students of these languages. The type to be selected for elementary German books should be bold and clear, and should mark the differences between certain similar letters. There are few German letters which present any difficulty.

When *reading* German from type (Frakturdruck) teach the distinctions between eu and en, ie and ei, b and d, f and ſ, r and x, B and V, M and W, T and J, R, V and K, the confusion of which gives rise sometimes to amusing mistakes in reading, e.g. ſchlendern for ſchleudern, Beleibtheit for Beliebtheit, Lied for Leid, Wein for Wien, ſein lieblicher Sohn for ſein leiblicher Sohn, Kinderpeſt for Rinderpeſt, der heilige Kater, der Randidat, ſaugen for fangen, ſaufen for ſauſen, Säugerin for Sängerin, Lüſtchen for Lüftchen, Bettel for Vettel, Art for Art, etc. All the other letters are easy[1]. When *writing* German insist on your pupils noting the modification of vowels and of au (äu, and not aü), the u hooks, and the difference between ß, ſ, ff, ß, and when writing Latin characters call the attention of your pupils to the fact that English and German Latin characters are not always the same, especially in the case of capital T and J.

The new Imperial Spelling of 1902 should certainly be adopted. It can very easily be taught, and it prevails now in

---

[1] Cp. the useful word-lists in O. Siepmann's excellent 'Public School German Primer,' London, Macmillan, ²1902, pp. xxvii—xxx, which afford ample reading practice.

all German schools and is used by most publishers and nearly all the newspapers. It will soon be found in the dictionaries[1]. It is decidedly the spelling of the future, being a moderate reform on the right lines, but no revolution of the traditional spelling. It is not ideal, but it is without doubt better than anything to be met with in the seventies or eighties of the last century, and certainly much better than the previous anarchy in spelling. There is, moreover, no reason why at some future time the present official orthography should not be revised again. The best books of reference for teachers are named on pp. 139—140 and in my *Handy Guide to the Study of German*, pp. 34, 51. To these should now be added, Johann Meyer: 'Die Abweichungen der neuen von der alten Rechtschreibung, nebst Übungsaufgaben, Diktaten, und einem Wörterverzeichnis. Für den Schul- und Selbstunterricht bearbeitet.' Hannover und Berlin, 1902, 20 pp. (3*d.*).

German Pronunciation.

The most elementary teaching—the laying of a good foundation—should invariably be entrusted to a carefully trained and thoroughly qualified master. He should be well acquainted with the elements of phonetics and should have a good pronunciation; he should have been abroad and should go again from time to time. He should know the principal differences of pronunciation in different parts of the country and should be acquainted with the chief shortcomings of the colloquial Hanoverian, Saxon, Swabian, and Berlin pronunciation[2]. He should have carefully considered what pronunciation he will teach, and what the standard of refined German speech requires[3].

[1] It is now given in the English-German portion of Cassell's 'New German Dictionary' (London, 1906).

[2] See pages 97—8 and 109.

[3] See 'German as she is spoke' (*Journal of Educ.*, 1897, pp. 533 sqq.), and pages 109 and 140—2 of this book.

The present standard pronunciation of Modern German is the pronunciation of the best actors on the stage[1]. Here a common pronunciation is absolutely necessary. A play like 'Iphigenie' would be completely spoilt if Orestes were to speak Swabian, Pylades Westphalian, Iphigenie Saxon, and King Thoas East Prussian. While the forms of the literary language are a compromise between South and Middle German, their pronunciation should be in the main North German. The pronunciation of refined Berlin ladies, who will never be heard to say *Jenuß, jlicklich*, or *Bealina* (= Berliner), *Brandenbuaja* (= Brandenburger), is particularly recommended. The Hanoverian pronunciation—excellent as it is in many respects—is not free from a number of provincialisms which should not be imitated. A teacher should beware of acquiring the Saxon pronunciation, the defects of which are especially marked.

The German text to be explained should invariably be read out once or twice by the master before his pupils read it to him. He should prepare this reading most carefully. In reading or reciting he should not only pronounce the individual words correctly, but give to the sentences their proper accentuation and modulation. Professor W. Viëtor's little book on 'German Pronunciation' (pp. 112—133, Leipzig, [2]1903) will help him to catch the proper accent of the sentence.

The use of the phonograph—strongly advocated by me in lectures for many years—will be found a great help in this. There are now three sets of German records, spoken by me, in Mrs Frazer's series [Cambridge Phonographic Records, records 95—130]. A talking machine (see p. 21) is useful for the teaching of the right intonation and also for precision. Experiments with the gramophone have also been made for English by the Langenscheidt firm of Berlin, and for foreign languages by Professor Rippmann in London.

None of these is as yet absolutely perfect, but some of the

---

[1] See pages 97—9.

records have been found very useful in class teaching, and others, while not yet sufficiently good for use with large forms, will yet be found useful for the private study of teachers and students. Probably it will not be long before the records and machines will be materially improved[1].

A new talking machine which claims to be much superior to the present phonograph and gramophone is called the Phonodidakt. I have not yet been able to test its merits. Information about it may be obtained from the Phonodaktische Gesellschaft, apply to die Expedition der 'Neueren Sprachen,' Marburg a/L.

Occasional readings, recitations, and theatrical performances by well qualified foreigners are now much encouraged in many German schools, and should if possible be secured for English boys and girls.

In some cases of special difficulty resort may well be had to a simple method of phonetic transcription of German words and sentences, such as is used by Professor Viëtor[2] in the latest edition of his 'Deutsche Lauttafel' or Professor Rippmann's new 'Sound Charts,' published by Dent (which should be hung up in the class-room during German lessons), or in Dr Passy's periodical publication 'Le maître phonétique.'

The following is a rough tabulated summary of the chief difficulties experienced by English-speaking children in pronouncing German.

---

[1] See my lecture on the use of the phonograph for the teaching of modern languages reported in the 'Cambridge Chronicle' of Aug. 17, 1906, which has been printed in full in *Die Neueren Sprachen*, Vol. xv, Heft 2.

[2] Unfortunately up to now no large sound chart is obtainable for school use in which the sounds of German are given in the transcription of the Association Phonétique Internationale. In the German and French sound charts published by Elwert of Marburg, the French has now the transcription of the A. P. I. About the aim and publications of the International Phonetic Association apply to Daniel Jones, Esq., 7, Copse Hill, Wimbledon. Rippmann's useful Charts cost 1s. net for each language.

The chief difficulties of German pronunciation[1], experienced by English-speaking pupils[2].

1. **ă** as in *Mann, Hals, hart, Anfang, Armband.*

Pupils should be accustomed to open their mouths wide in pronouncing this sound, which is the *a* in Northern Engl. *father*, but quite short and slightly more open. The sound is heard in English unstressed *are*. It is not the sound of the English *a* in *hat*, viz. *danken* must not be pronounced like *denken*.

2. **ī, ē, ō, ū**, especially before *r*, as in *ihr, Lehm, rot, Rohr, fuhr.*

Here the difficulty lies in the necessity of producing a long *uniform* vowel, without sounding a second element after it, e.g. *vier* is not to be pronounced like *fear*, *Lehm* not like *lame*, *Rohr* not like *roar*, *rot* not like *wrote*, *pur* not like *poor*. The lips should be well rounded in pronouncing long closed *o* and *u*.

3. **ŏ̈, ō̈, ŭ̈, ṻ, ǟ** as in *Hölle, Höhle; fülle, fühle; wäre.*

The modified vowels *ö*, *ü* (short and open—long and closed) do not exist in English and consequently require special practice. The long closed *ö* (in phonetic script *ø:*) requires very careful practice in words such as *König, Söhne, schön*, etc. *Goethe* (*gø:tə*) should not be pronounced *gətə*. Again teachers should not allow pupils to say *fu:r* instead of *für*, or *funf* instead of *fünf*, etc., but they should at the outset give the class a brief and clear phonetic explanation of the position of the speech organs in sounding *ü* and *ö*, and should practise these sounds whenever an opportunity occurs. The

[1] The symbols used are largely those of the Association Phonétique Internationale. Cp. the useful observations in W. Rippmann's *Hints on Teaching German*. The following remarks do not lay any claim to completeness. See now W. Viëtor, ' Deutsches Lesebuch in Lautschrift,' Leipzig, Part I, [2]1904, Part II, 1902, and his ' Deutsches Aussprachewörterbuch' with phonetic transcriptions, Leipzig, 1908, now in course of publication. See also D. L. Savory, 'Deutsches Reformlesebuch,' Oxford, 1908, where the words (in the glossary) are given in phonetic script ; and p. 141.

[2] See the Cambridge Phonographic Records, Nos. 95 and 107.

best way of doing this is to allow the pupils first to pronounce the simple sounds *i* and *e*, and then show them that by keeping the tongue in the same position and gradually rounding the lips, the more difficult *ü* and *ö* sounds are obtained, thus, *Hindin—Hündin, Nixlein—Füchslein, sehnen—(ver)söhnen, Helle—Hölle.* They may like to use my phonographic records Nos. 95 and 107 in Mrs Frazer's series. They should also point out the difference in the sound of the vowels in *wäre* and *wary*, *Käfer* and *chafer*, *Ähre* and *airy*, *Ähre* and *Ehre*, *Säle* and *Seele*, and so forth, and they should make it clear that there is no difference in pronunciation between *ai* and *ei*, e.g. *Seite* and *Saite* are both pronounced *zaitǝ*.

4. **au** as in *rauschen, heraus, auch, Raum.*

The mouth should be opened sufficiently for the *a* element of the diphthong, which is also longer than in English, while the tongue is, as a rule, not raised in front. The second element resembles more an open *o* than a *u*, which fact is not expressed in the phonetic transcription adopted by the Association Phonétique Internationale, which renders *au* by *au* (not *a:ɔ*) and *ai* or *ei* by *ai* (not *a:ɛ*).

5. **a** in unaccented syllables is to be distinctly pronounced, e.g. *Komm*a (not like *kommǝ*), *Ann*a, *Fuld*a, *Walhall*a, *Eil*and.

e in unaccented syllables is nearly always reduced to a dull *ǝ*, e.g. *behende* should be pronounced *bǝ'hɛndǝ*; *nehmen* is *'ne:mǝn*; *Hameln* is *'ha:mǝln*; *Kindern* is *'kindǝrn*; *Oberst* is *'ʔo:bǝrst*; *gegeben* is *gǝ'ge:bǝn*; *Ehre is 'ʔe:rǝ*; *Ehe* is *'ʔe:ǝ*; *eilend* is *'ʔailǝnt*, but *Elend* (which stands for *Ellend*, O. H. G. *elilenti* 'foreign land,' 'exile,' subsequently 'wretchedness') is *'ʔe:lɛnt*.

In final **-er** the *r* should be clearly sounded; many mistakes in dictation occur from the failure on the part of the scholars to distinguish between such words as *Bürge—Bürger, Schiffe—Schiffer, Städte—Städter, Türme—Türmer, Apotheke—Apotheker, ehe—eher; Herder* is not *Hörde*, etc.

In familiar pronunciation, which is not to be imitated in reading poetry or high style prose, the *e* in unaccented syllables usually disappears after *b*, *d*, *g*, e.g. *leben* becomes *le : bᵐ*, *Odem* becomes *o : dᵐ*, *sieden* becomes *zi : dⁿ*, *tragen* becomes *tra : gŋ*, or *danken* becomes *daŋkŋ*. See p. 72, under 11.

6. **The glottal stop** before the initial vowel, even if the word is the second part of a compound, should be carefully noticed and practised, see p. 19. Thus *Goldammer* should be pronounced *'gɔltʔamər*; *umarmen* is *um'ʔarmən*, *vereinigen* is *fər'ʔainigən*, *allüberall* is *'ʔalʔy:bər'ʔal*, *Glückauf* is *glyk'ʔauf*, etc. Distinguish between *Baumast* and *Baumeister*, *Dreimaster*; *Postamt* and *Postament*, *uralt* and *Uralsee*, etc. The glottal stop should also be noticed in *Weltall*; *Rührei*; *Hühnerei*; *Treibeis*; *Tierarzt*; *Denkart*; *Sonnenuhr*, etc.

7. **h** is now absolutely silent between vowels, as in *sahen*, except in compounds (*Hoheit, Roheit*), where English children are inclined to drop it. It is sometimes sounded in this country in artificial school pronunciation. *Wehen* is to be pronounced *'ve:ən*, *ziehen* is *'tsi:ən*, *Ehe* is *'ʔe:ə*, *nahe* is *'na:ə*, *gedeihen* is *gə'daiən*, etc.

8. Final **b**, **d**, even when at the end of the first part of a compound, are to be pronounced as voiceless sounds (*p, t*). Hence *Held* is *hɛlt*, *Gold* is *gɔlt*, *weiblich* is *vaipliç*.

b and *d* after a consonant do *not* lengthen the preceding vowel in German : e.g. *Hand* is *hant*, *Mund* is *munt*, *derb* is *dɛrp*. Exceptions are *Mo:nt*, *Pfɛ:rt*, *wɛ:rt*, and others.

9. **w** has the sound of *v*, not that of English *w* (although the German *w* has less friction than the English *v*), e.g. *wichsen* ('to black boots') is *'viksən*. English children should be careful to distinguish between such words as *Wetter* and *Vetter*, *Wolke* and *Volke*. After *sch*, *w* is either bilabial (but without any rounding of the lips), or labio-dental (*v*). Most authorities now recommend the latter (*v*) pronunciation[1]. Thus *schwarz* is *ʃvarts*, *Schwein* is *ʃvain*.

---

[1] See Siebs, *Bühnenaussprache*, [2]1901, p. 59, and Viëtor, *German Pronunciation*, [3]1903, pp. 40—1.

10. **u** after *q* has likewise the (bilabial or) labio-dental sound (*qu = kv*), e.g. *Quell* is *kvɛl*, *Qual* is *kva:l*, *quälen* is *'kvɛ:lən*, *quer* is *kve:r* [not *kuɛl, kua:l, kuɛ:lən, kue:r*].

11. **The guttural n** before *g* and *k* when followed by a vowel must also be noted. *g* following *n* is never sounded in German, but invariably turns the *n* into a guttural (*ŋ*), there is in German no instance of a pronunciation like the English *fiŋgər* (for *finger*), nor of the uneducated English *darlin* or *darlink* (for *darling*).

The guttural *n* is usually transcribed *ŋ*, sometimes *ŋ*. The German *Finger* is pronounced *'fiŋər*, *singen* is *'ziŋən*, while *sinken* is *'ziŋkən*. The pronunciation of words such as *Engel* —*Enkel*, *Range*—*Ranke*, *Sang*—*sank*, *Drang*—*Trank*, *bang* —*Bank*, *sengen*—*senken*, *längen*—*lenken*, etc. should be practised. If the *n* preceding the *g* is the final letter of a prefix or of the first part of a compound, the *g* must of course be sounded, e.g. *angehn* is *'ʔange:n*, while *bangen* must be pronounced *'baŋən*. Cp. also *drangen* and *drangehn*, *Angel* and *angelernt*, *Bengel* and *Bengalen*.

12. The peculiar German **ch** has a twofold pronunciation after front and back vowels, e.g. *lächeln* is *'lɛçəln*, but *lachen* is *'laχən*, cp. also *ich* and *doch*, cp. Scotch '*loch*'; *Früchte, Frucht*; *Töchter, Tochter*; *rächen, Rache*.

The English child will need to be carefully taught not to say *ish, ik, ak*, etc. The pronunciation of the front, or palatal, *ch* may be taught by making the pupils first say the English word *yearn*, then say it as if the *y* were voiceless. This gives the front *ch* sound initially and by saying *i-yearn* (still with the voiceless *y*), the final and medial front *ch* is obtained. In *hue* the sound is often heard following the *h*.

As *ch* may be sounded differently in forms of the same word (e.g. *Buch*—*Bücher*), great care is necessary in practising the pronunciation. The sounds *cht* and *gt* must also be carefully distinguished, or confusion between such words as (*ihr*) *wāgt*—*wacht*, *sāgt*—*sacht*, *liegt*—*Licht* will arise.

13. **z** in German words (and **c** in certain foreign loan words) is a consonant diphthong denoting *ts*, as in *fits* and *starts*. Pupils should be early accustomed to pronounce it well (neither like *s* nor *dz*). Thus a clear distinction must be made between *Seiten* and *Zeiten*, *sauber* and *Zauber*, *säugen* and *zeugen*, *gesogen* and *gezogen*, *Saum* and *Zaum*, *sehen* and *Zehen*, *unselige* and *unzählige*, *Schweiß* and *Schweiz* (*ſvaits*), *Sehne*, *Zähne* and *Szene* (=′*stse* : *nə*), *Siege* and *Ziege*, *Selbstsucht* and *Selbstzucht*, *Sinn* and *Zinn* (in order to avoid writing sentences like ' Das kommt mir nicht aus dem *Zinn*' !), *Seile* and *Zeile* (In diesen *Seilen* liegt tiefe Wahrheit), *reisend*, *reissend* and *reizend*, etc.; *zwanzig* must be pronounced ′*tsvantsiç*.

14. Initial **sp** and **st**, even at the beginning of the second part of a compound, should be pronounced *ſp*, *ſt*, as it is on the stage and in the greater part of Germany. The change in pronunciation of *s* to *sch* (in phonetic script *ſ*) before *p* and *t* should take place just as it has taken place before *l*, *m*, *n*, *w* all over the country, e.g. *sleht* > *schlecht*, *smerz* > *Schmerz*, *snel* > *schnell*, *swîn* > *Schwein*. The North-West German (e.g. Hanoverian) pronunciation is, in this case, archaic and obviously influenced by Low German. The retention of the obsolete spelling in words such as *sprechen* and *streiten* must be accounted for by the desire not to write *schprechen* and *schtreiten*. Hence *sprechen* should be ′*ſprɛçən*, *gestehen* should be *gə′ſte* : *ən* ; but the South German pronunciation of medial and final *st* as *ſt* should not be imitated, e.g. *Meister* should *not* be pronounced ′*maiſtər*, *bist* not *bi* : *ſt*, *hast* not *hɔſt*, *Oberst* not ′*ʔo* : *bərſt*. Plenty of practice should be given to beginners, and groups of words should be given and discussed such as *Austern*, *Ostern*, *Fixstern*, *beste*, *bestehen*, *Gäste*, *gestehen*, etc.

Dialectic pronunciation may indeed be found in the works of the great German writers ; Schiller, for instance, never freed himself from his strong Swabian accent, and we frequently find in his poems a confusion between the voiced and voiceless sibilants, in the rimes *Rose* (=*ro* : *zə*) and *Schoße* (=*ſo* : *sə*)

which he pronounced *Schose* (=*ʃo*:*zə*)[1].   For the same reason
Goethe pronounced and dictated the name of the village in
which he met the charming Friederike Brion (in 1770)
Sesenheim, although its official spelling is *Sessenheim*.   Its
present local Alsatian pronunciation is *Säsm*. This confusion of
the voiced and voiceless hissing sounds is a South and Middle
German characteristic.

A number of smaller points might still be touched upon,
such as the difference between the thinner and clear German
and the fuller and dark English *l* (cp. *voll* and *full*, *Kessel* and
kettle), but the space at my disposal does not admit a discussion
of them, and these hints must not become a treatise.   The
books and pamphlets by Viëtor, Siebs, Rippmann, Miss Soames,
Braune and Johannson[2] will give teachers all the necessary
information as to particular points.   A teacher of German will
do well to consult them in cases of difficulty or doubt.

Open Questions.

The pronunciation of initial and medial *r* (lingual or guttural)
and of medial and final *g* are moot points with the Germans
themselves.   I should allow a good deal of latitude in the
teaching of them, that is to say, I should not force English
children to learn the guttural *r* if it gives them much trouble,
as, for example, in the word *rühren*.   Lingual *r* is heard everywhere in Germany both on the stage and in the concert room.
I should advocate the teaching of medial *g* between vowels as
a voiced mute and not as a spirant.   Hence I should transcribe
Wege as *'ve*:*gə* (not *'ve*:*jə*).   Medial *g* before *t* also should
be a voiceless mute, e.g. *er siegt*, not *er siecht* ('conquers,' *not*
'languishes from disease') (*'zi*:*kt*, not *'zi*:*çt*).   About final *g*

[1] See the interesting account of it given by E. Genast, *Aus Weimars
klassischer und nachklassischer Zeit. Erinnerungen eines alten Schauspielers*
(ed. by Robert Kohlrausch[3], I. p. 69).   Schiller pronounced *ʃo*:*zə*.
[2] See the lists given on pages 127 and 140—2.

I do not feel so sure, and should (at present) admit the pronunciation *ve:k* or *ve:ç* for *Weg*. The latter (*ve:ç*) is the more familiar one and is more generally heard; it seems to be the pronunciation of the future. Hence perhaps the best plan for the present is to pronounce final *g* hard in high style and in poetry, as it is pronounced on the stage (see Siebs, *Bühnenaussprache*, ²1901, p. 76), but as a spirant in reading ordinary prose, and in conversation. At all events the *g* in words such as *möglich, tauglich* is in ordinary German almost always pronounced as a spirant, and in school teaching it seems more natural to adopt this pronunciation. In the suffix *-ig* the final *g* is spirantic, e.g. *ewig* is *'ʔe:viç*; *ewige* is *'ʔe:vigə*, while *ew'ge* should be pronounced *'ʔe:vjə*. If followed by *-lich* the *g* is always hard, e.g. *ewiglich* is *'ʔe:vikliç*[1]. The *g* in foreign words is sometimes hard and sometimes soft: *Logik, Logis*; *Genius* and *Genie* are easy examples. The pronunciation of *g* in such words consequently requires some attention. But it can in most cases be mastered without any difficulty by following a simple rule.

Grammar.

The few words I propose to say under this head are entirely dictated by the practical considerations of school teaching. The general principles have been discussed on pages 25 sqq., e.g. that only the chief facts of grammar should be taught, and everything exceptional at first be eliminated; also that grammar should not be taught at school for its own sake, and that everything should be as far as possible deduced from carefully chosen examples of good modern German which would mainly be prose.

[1] See Th. Siebs, *Bühnenaussprache*, ²1901, p. 76, iv. A new edition will soon be published. See also the introductory remarks to W. Viëtor's new *Aussprachewörterbuch* (1908).

What is the standard ? I think the usage of first-rate modern writers such as Heyse, Spielhagen, Wildenbruch, Storm, Ompteda, Polenz, Stratz, Geibel, Bodenstedt, Fulda, and others. But teachers should be careful in the use of examples from Freytag, Scheffel, Keller, Raabe, Rosegger, Sudermann, Hauptmann and others whose writings are not free from archaisms, mannerisms, dialectic usages and even a good deal of slang. These writings may be great works of art, but they cannot be used with beginners because they cannot be held up without reservation as models of refined modern prose.

Nearly all the existing grammars of German compiled for the use of English schools have serious defects in addition to those general shortcomings noted on pages 27—8 :

(1) They do not sufficiently distinguish between familiar, ordinary and historical, and elevated modern prose.

(2) They do not as a rule distinguish carefully enough between prose and poetry.

(3) They do not generally distinguish between the modern language and the language of the great 18th century classics. In many cases we cannot say and write now what Lessing, Goethe, and Schiller could say and write. The teacher might point out this difference, giving also a few examples at random illustrating the different use of certain words in the writings of the classics, e.g. Lessing's *Ausschweifung* for the present-day *Abschweifung*, *galant* for *elegant*, Goethe's use of *Ankunft* for *Abkunft*, his peculiar use of *dumpf* and *bedeutend*, the older uses of *Witz* and *Wollust*, and many others.

Thus a prevalent fault is the failure to distinguish between the cases used in connection with certain verbs, e.g. *entbehren*, *rufen*, *genießen*, etc. It is absolutely misleading to say, as most grammars and dictionaries do, '*entbehren* takes either the gen. or the acc.' It is true that Hermann (in 'Hermann und Dorothea,' written in 1797) says : *Ich entbehre der Gattin*, but it is archaic and cannot be said now. In good modern prose the accusative is used exclusively. Again in the case of *rufen* the accusative is now the only possible case, e.g. *er ruft mich*. The dative which occurs sometimes in an elevated style, and which is still used in South Germany and Switzerland, is very expressive, e.g. when the Spirit of the Earth calls out to Faust *Wer ruft mir?* 'Who calls *for* me?' But such rare or dialectic or poetic constructions should be briefly explained when they happen to occur in the text read by the pupils.

Hence the instances from the German classics in most of our grammars require a very thorough overhauling. A teacher should know modern literary and colloquial German very well himself, so as not to be hopelessly dependent on the grammar he happens to use.

A good teacher should not only teach the dry facts of grammar, but sometimes in appropriate cases give an explanation. I have cautioned teachers not to go too far (see page 29), but now and then they may well give some colour to their teaching by supplying an easy explanation, e.g. on the origin of many German prepositions, *kraft—laut—wegen—während—mittels(t)* (why are they followed by the genitive?), or of adverbs: *flugs—rings—spornstreichs—allerdings*, etc. A word on the nouns in *-ei* and the ending *-ieren* in verbs would interest many of the older boys, as would one on doublets such as *Kerker* and *Karzer*, *Ferien* and *Feier*, *Partie* and *Partei*, *Bursch* and *Börse*, *dichten* and *diktieren*. Even the inorganic *t* in *eigentlich*, *geflissentlich*, after the analogy of *hoffentlich*, *flehentlich* (for *flehend-lich* 'like one imploring'), the inorganic *s* in *Reitersmann*, *Hoffnungsstrahl*, and similar cases, might occasionally be explained to advanced pupils. They will thus get a glimpse of the life of the language. There is no lack of handy books of reference for the teacher of German who is anxious to obtain fuller information[1].

---

[1] See pages 138—9: 'The Reference Library of a School Teacher of German.'

But be very careful that your pupils do not use any scientific terms *without properly understanding their exact meaning and their full bearing.* Do not allow them to explain away difficulties by one of the four ever-recurring phrases:

'for the sake of euphony,'

'by false analogy' (with what? why false?),

'by poetic licence,' or, 'for the sake of the metre,'

as if Goethe or Schiller could not have managed their versification properly! Do not permit them to think that the *n* in Sonne*n*schein was 'added,' and the *d* in Montag 'omitted' '*for the sake of euphony*'! They should not be allowed to prefix a statement about which they feel extremely doubtful, by a bold 'of course,' or to use the favourite phrase 'more or less,' e.g. 'these lines rime more or less.'

I have said that a good teacher will take pains to find out the chief difficulties of his pupils and will work hard at these while he will pass quickly over things which are naturally easy to English children.

Some of the *principal* difficulties of German grammar seem to me:

(1) *The right use of the prepositions*[1] and of the cases required in connection with them. Many grammars are not adequate in this respect, e.g. the short rule as to 'rest' and 'motion' is misleading in the case of prepositions with two cases. The right use of the prepositions is a great, perhaps the greatest difficulty, and can only be mastered by dint of constant practice and observation[2]. Still I am firmly convinced that

---

[1] Cp. the original illustrated pamphlet 'German prepositions at a glance,' by C. Kaiser and A. Thouaille of the Gouin School of Languages, 35 Bold Street, Liverpool.

[2] It would perhaps be a good plan if the children had grammar note-books with suitable headings to each page. The examples would be entered as they occur, e.g. *über* : Er steht über den Parteien—Der Ballon schwebt über der Stadt—Der Wind treibt den Ballon über die Stadt—Er schreibt über das Theater ; *auf*: Er sitzt auf der Bank—Er steigt auf die Bank—Die Ente schwimmt auf dem Teich—Er schilt auf die Zeitungen.—

a skilful teacher will be able to train his pupils in the right use
of the prepositions to such an extent that by the time they
leave school not one of the ordinary common mistakes will be
made by any scholar.

(2) *The inflexion of the adjectives.* The threefold use of
the adjective (strong and weak inflexion and uninflected form)
is characteristic of the German language. This difficulty should,
however, soon be overcome—a number of typical instances
will suffice to teach it. These examples should be gathered
from the Reader and learned by heart. Cases such as
*auf gut Glück, bar Geld, Röslein rot, vom Himmel hoch
da komm' ich her, in jung und alten Tagen, nach solchen
Opfern, heilig großen, mit neuem kölnischen Wasser,* and others
should be briefly discussed when they first occur.

(3) *The modifications of root-vowels* in plurals, comparisons,
and derivatives. Here a careful pronunciation will be of great
help—but much must simply be learned by heart, e.g. *Tag,
Tage,* but *Schlag, Schläge* ; *Hund, Hunde,* but *Grund, Gründe,
Laut, Laute,* but *Haut, Häute.*

(4) The principal types of *declensions*, strong and weak.

(5) The *strong verbs* ; the *separable verbs*.

The principal ones must be committed to memory ; comparison with English (*singe, sang, gesungen : sing, sang, sung*)
will in many cases be helpful, and will at all events remind
pupils that a verb may be strong. In the case of reflexive
verbs the *first person*, and not the infinitive, should be learned ;
thus *ich fürchte mich, ich denke mir* (not *sich fürchten, sich denken*),
*ich nehme mich in acht, ich stelle mir vor, ich bilde mir ein, ich
erinnere mich, ich bin mir bewusst, ich mache mir Gedanken,* etc.
The most important of these should be entered in the pupil's

When there are enough examples the children, with the help of the teacher,
deduce the rules themselves, and may afterwards be constantly referred back
to them. See W. Rippmann, *Hints on the teaching of German,* p. 59,
where this is worked out in detail, and see also Rippmann's *New First
German Book,* p. 138.

note-book and committed to memory. In the case of the separable and inseparable verbs the principal ones, but only the principal ones, should be learned early, and a good pronunciation should be insisted upon. Here again the first persons *ich setze über*, 'I put across,' and *ich übersétze*, 'I translate,' should be employed in class-teaching instead of the infinitives (*ü'bersetzen, überse'tzen*).

Pupils should be told that as a rule in cases where the force of the preposition is still felt and a local meaning prevails the verb is separable, but that it is inseparable where its equivalent is not a true English verb plus a preposition or adverb, but a compound borrowed from Latin or Romance and where the meaning is abstract. Thus *übersetzen* 'put across,' *übersétzen* 'translate'; *wiéderholen* 'fetch back,' *wiederhólen* 'repeat'; *dúrchgehen* 'go through,' *durchgéhen* 'pervade'; *úmgehen* 'go round about,' *umgéhen* 'circumvent,' etc.

(6) *The order of words in a sentence.* This is of the very greatest importance and causes a great deal of difficulty at first, but the chief points can perfectly well be learned at school. The chief cases of inversion should be explained at an early stage and constantly (and methodically) practised for several weeks—then they will probably cause little trouble at later stages. Begin early with very simple sentences, enlarge them, alter them and turn them about, gradually introducing the various kinds of dependent clauses. Make your own examples if necessary, let the children copy them, and refer at first invariably to the same examples until the *Sprachgefühl* of the pupils is sufficiently well developed. Begin with a number of sentences such as .

> *Ich kenne den Knaben.*
> I know the boy.
> *Der Knabe, welchen ich kenne.*
> The boy whom I know.
> *Das Mädchen findet das Buch.*
> The girl finds the book.

Das Mädchen hat das Buch gefunden.
The girl has found the book.

Many instances of a similar kind should be given before you go on, always adding a little:

Das [schöne] Mädchen, [welches wir (heute) sahen], hat seinen [guten] Vater verloren, etc. etc.

Invent a story or a fable, and embody in it the chief things you are anxious to illustrate, e.g. the principal differences between English and German syntax. Let this be written down and learned by heart and refer to it again and again when mistakes have occurred. By means of frequent repetition the memory will be trained and at last the teacher's highest aim will be attained—the development of *Sprachgefühl* on the part of the pupil. See page 28.

Genders.

The German genders are certainly very troublesome to foreigners, e.g. *der Rest, die Pest, das Fest, Nest; der Ast, Gast, Mast, die Hast, Last; die Bewandtnis, das Gefängnis; Der Monat, die Heimat; der Hochmut, die Armut; der Rat, Vorrat, die Heirat; die Saat, Naht, Tat; der Ornat, das Internat, Lektorat; der Schnee, See, die Fee, Idee, das Komitee; der Rüssel, Schlüssel, die Schüssel; der Wein, Schein, die Pein, das Bein; der Bauer, Hauer, Schauer, die Mauer, Trauer, das Bauer, Schauer; der Mut, die Wut, das Blut; der Rost, Most, die Post, Kost,* etc. etc. Unfortunately there are not many good rules about them. I wish there were. I cannot say more than the grammars. Historical and etymological explanations are as a rule out of place in school teaching. The teacher will probably explain the reason why *Mädchen* and *Fräulein* are neuters, but the reason for the neuter gender of *Weib* is beyond the information to be given at school. I freely admit that children, while at school, cannot be expected to acquire an absolutely correct knowledge of genders, especially of the genders of unusual synonymous words, e.g. *der Grashüpfer*, *die Grille*, *das Heupferd*, and I should certainly be much more annoyed by a bad mistake in pronunciation than by a mistake about the gender of a less familiar word. On the other hand I do not think that the genders are quite as hard as they are sometimes made out to be. In the amusing chapter 'On the awful German language' added to his delightful 'Tramp abroad,' Mark Twain has with a great deal of humour exaggerated the difficulties. I think that even school-children may not unreasonably be expected to know the genders of *all* or *nearly all* the German words of everyday occurrence. Here the 'systematic vocabulary' referred to on pages 31 sqq. should be useful, and more the school cannot be expected to give.

Die Sonne—der Mond—der Stern—die Wolke—der Nebel, etc. In learning words children should not say *Sonne—Mond* but *die Sonne—der Mond*, always adding the definite article and perhaps an ordinary qualifying adjective, e.g. *Die liebe Sonne*, *der gute Mond, der helle Stern, die schwarze Wolke, der warme Regen, der heulende Wind, der dichte Nebel, der glänzende Schnee, das glatte Eis*, etc. A story might be made up by the teacher which he should first tell and then dictate to the class. The pupils would learn it by heart and could, in case of subsequent doubts or mistakes, be referred back to it. An account of a ramble in the country might end as follows : 'Der Gipfel des Berges war bald erstiegen. Von ihm sahen wir die Sonne untergehen und bald nach ihrem Untergang den Mond und den Abendstern am Himmel aufgehen. Eine düstre Wolke verbarg uns den schönen Stern auf kurze Zeit, ein starkes Gewitter zog herauf, ein greller Blitz folgte dem andern, der Donner rollte, der Regen floß in Strömen ; bald aber war das schwere Wetter vorbei gezogen, der Himmel wieder klar, von der Wiese stieg der weiße Nebel empor, und das Licht des freundlichen Sternes leuchtete wieder zu uns herab.' Or the following slightly more difficult piece, containing many of the ordinary terms connected with the sea, might be dictated and discussed : 'Hans,

Hans, wo bist du? Beeile dich! Komm schnell auf Deck! In fünf Minuten fahren wir ab und hinaus auf das Meer, das ruhig und dunkel vor uns liegt. Ich sehe einige Lichter weit hinten auf dem Wasser, und links das helle Licht des Leuchtturms oben auf der Klippe. Horch, die Glocke tönt, die Laufbrücke wird zurückgezogen, und die Schiffspfeife giebt das Zeichen zur Abfahrt. Die Anker werden gelichtet, die schweren Ketten rasseln, jeder Matrose ist auf seinem Posten, und oben auf der Kommandobrücke steht der Kapitän. Langsam verlässt unser Dampfer die Landestelle. Vorsichtig gleitet er durch die kleineren Fahrzeuge, welche im Hafen vor Anker liegen, und steuert in dunkler Nacht hinaus auf das offne Meer. Sieh, wie freundlich die Lichter der Stadt noch zu uns herüberblitzen! Der Strahl, welcher uns plötzlich trifft, kommt von dem elektrischen Scheinwerfer des Forts dort oben. Nun aber sind wir weit vom Lande entfernt, die Lichter verschwinden, und das Kommando erschallt "Volldampf voraus!" Lass uns noch ein wenig auf Deck bleiben und plaudern; wenn morgen früh die Sonne aufgeht, werden wir die holländische Küste vor uns sehen.'

Word-formation.

Only the most important facts of German word-formation (derivation and composition and the old formation by vowel gradation) should be taught, but word-formation will naturally play an important part in the construing lessons and will be sure to interest the children if it is properly brought before them. They should be told why er*inn*ern has one *r* and two *n*'s, and should be informed that Inte*r*esse has one *r* and is not connected with *enterrer*. Some philological knowledge will be indispensable to a teacher of even ordinary German[1]. He might show, for instance, the importance of noticing older case-

---

[1] See pages 103—8.

forms in word-formation, e.g. *Sonnenschein, Frauenkirche, Gänsefeder, Hahnenkamm, Bräutigam, Bürgemeister, Heidenröslein, Nasenbein, Pfauenfeder*, etc. A well-informed teacher may also profitably now and then explain the formation of a word with a view to giving the pupils a glimpse of old German life, customs, and beliefs. The discussion of the names of the days of the week, e.g. *Donnerstag* and *Freitag*, words such as *Ostern, Weihnachten, Fastnacht, Mahlstätte, Kurfürst, Hochzeit, Brautlauf* (in Schiller's 'Tell'), and of such verbs as *erfahren, verteidigen, sich entschließen*, would be sure to interest and instruct the children. In saying this I am far from advocating a display of etymological information which would be beyond the understanding of the children and altogether out of place in school teaching. Again an occasional word as to family names such as Baumann, Agricola, Münch, Thurn, Gottschall, Wigand, Wurmb, Jacobi, Jacobssohn, Jacobs, or of German and foreign proper names, such as Dietrich, Leopold, Ludwig, Wolfram, Gottschalk, Götz, Gerhard, Reinhart, Rudolf, Walter, Minna, Adelheid, Gertrud, Hedwig—Andreas, Philipp, Moses, Ludovica, Louise—Wolfgang Weber and Elisabeth Textor, Lurlei, Lorelei, Rübezahl, or names of towns and countries, such as Aachen, Köln, Koblenz, Braunschweig, München, Frankfurt, Weißenburg, Wittenberg, Marienwerder, Sachsen, Sigmaringen, Lothringen, Staufer, Hohenstaufen, Hohenzollern, Habsburg (not Hapsburg), Welfen, etc. could be made most interesting and valuable even to children. Their attention might also be drawn to English names of the same old stock, e.g. Hilda, Mildred, Winifred, Alfred, Harold. The teacher might say a word about *prefixes* in English and German, e.g. *G*laube—*b*elief; *be*reit—ready; *be*gleiten, *ab*gleiten—*be*gleitet, *ab*geglitten, etc. Attention should be called to the German spelling and pronunciation of Elisabeth [ʔeːˈliːzaːbɛt], Phi*l*ipp [ˈfiːlip], and Emanuel [ʔeːˈmaːnuɛl], Immanuel [ˈʔimaːnuɛl]. Such instruction should, however, never be given systematically at school, but only as occasion offers.

I shall be much pleased if in these lectures on modern language teaching I have succeeded in throwing out some hints which will prove useful in your future work, and in firing your enthusiasm for a subject, the study and teaching of which grows more attractive and is being more fully developed with every year. You will soon be called upon to take your full share in it. The way is long, the aim is high—let us make a resolute attempt to reach the goal or at least not fall too far short of it!

THE TRAINING OF MODERN LANGUAGE
TEACHERS[1]

IF in the following pages I shall mainly confine myself
to the discussion of the training of a future teacher of German,
I trust that, *mutatis mutandis*, my remarks will be found
equally useful for intending teachers of French and other
modern languages. Nor shall I speak here of those general
qualifications which every good teacher of any subject must
possess, viz. culture, character, energy, tact in maintaining
discipline, and a thorough understanding of the minds of
young people, nor of the special professional training to be
obtained at some training department after the completion of a
student's academic course, but only propose to discuss the
special training of a modern language teacher, i.e. I shall only
speak of such qualifications as can be won by scientific and
practical training with regard to (1) language, (2) literature,
and (3) facts and studies illustrating these which, for the sake
of brevity, I shall in the following paragraphs call 'realia.'

A modern language master of the best type must, I believe,
(a) not only study the language and literature of the foreign

[1] This paper was originally printed in the 'Educational Times' of May,
1894. See now Viëtor's theses (in 'Die Neueren Sprachen,' Vol. XIV (1906–7),
pp. 290 sqq. and the note on p. 512) proposed in 1906 at Munich to the
members of the Allgemeiner Deutscher Neuphilologenverband; Viëtor's
brief but valuable summary 'Die Ausbildung der Neuphilologen' in the
Pädagogisches Archiv, Vol. L (1908); the Report on the training of Modern
Language teachers drawn up by a Special Committee of the Modern
Language Association, and published in the April number of *Modern
Language Teaching*.

nation for their own sake, but also by means of them the genius and civilization of that nation ; (*b*) gain his knowledge not only in Great Britain, but, to some extent, abroad; (*c*) overcome completely any shyness in speaking, free himself from all prejudice, look at what he sees not only from his own insular standpoint, but also from that of the foreigner, and judge of things and conditions as they present themselves to his mind.

'What is the best linguistic and literary training for a teacher of modern languages, and especially for a teacher of German, in secondary schools?'

It will be easiest, I think, to give a satisfactory answer to the above question, if we first agree as to what a competent teacher of a modern language should know. He must, I believe, (*a*) know the modern language thoroughly in its *present* condition; (*b*) be able to explain the chief linguistic and literary phenomena historically.

It is altogether wrong to oppose these two qualifications, as if the one excluded the other, or as if the empirical and the scientific mastery of a language must not of necessity supplement one another. Surely both are necessary and should go hand in hand. The past must be illustrated by the present, but no less the present by the past.

The study of German in the widest sense comprises the study of

(A) First, the living language, which may be subdivided into (*a*) the familiar (spoken) language (*Umgangssprache*); (*b*) the literary (written) language (*Schriftsprache*, also *Rednersprache*)—this requires a practical and scientific study; (*c*) a slight acquaintance with a few of the most striking peculiarities of some of the most important dialects, e.g. Low German, Saxon, Bavarian, or Alemannic. To the whole of the first division must be added the auxiliary study of phonetics.

(B) Secondly, it must embrace the *older phases of the language*, i.e. some selected Old and Middle High German texts, with the elements of O.H.G. and M.H.G. grammar.

(C)   Thirdly, *the history of the German language*.   In this country the connection with English should be pointed out everywhere.   As an auxiliary study I mention the outlines of the science of language and of comparative philology.

(D)   Fourthly, *literature*, comprising (*a*) the study of representative authors of different periods; (*b*) a historical survey of the development of literature, in which the manifold connections of German with English literature should especially be carefully noticed.   The principal auxiliary studies are: Out lines of (1) theory of metre; (2) theory of poetry.

(E)   Fifthly, *realia*, i.e. *illustrative facts and studies*, com-prising a study of German life and thought, customs, and institutions at different periods, but mainly those of the present time, to be partly acquired abroad by personal observation and experience.   The chief auxiliary studies are: history and geography[1].

The importance of most of the branches of study which I have mentioned is fully recognised, and consequently they

---

[1] Is it too much to expect that a teacher of German should be able to make clear to his pupils the significance of the term *das heilige römische Reich deutscher Nation* and the difference between the authority and the functions of the Hohenstaufen and Hohenzollern emperors?   What differ-ence is there between the *Sachsenkaiser* and the *Könige von Sachsen*? Why is William II called *deutscher Kaiser* and not *Kaiser von Deutsch-land*?   Who are *die Welfen* and *die Wittelsbacher*?   Who were *die Deutschherrn*?   What difference is there between a *Markgraf* and a *Pfalzgraf*?   Who was *der große Kurfürst*?   What does *die Mark Bran-denburg* mean? but where does *der Märker* live of whom Arndt sings (in *Was ist des Deutschen Vaterland?*): *Ist's, wo der Märker Eisen reckt?*   What are *eine Hansastadt, der Hanseat, der Belt*?   What difference is there between *Schlesien* and *Schleswig*?   What is meant by *der deutsche Krieg*? *die Mainlinie*? *die schwarz-weißroten* or *die blau-weißen Grenzpfähle*? *die rote Erde, die Waterkant, die Reichslande, die deutschen Mittelstaaten, ein Niedersachse*?   What is a *Krönungsstadt*?   What is a *freie Stadt* in modern Germany?   By whom is it governed and in what relation does it stand to the Empire?   What are the functions of the *Bundesrat, Reichstag, Herrenhaus, Abgeordnetenhaus, Reichsgericht, Reichskanzler?* etc.

do not require any comment. But, with regard to a few subjects, a general agreement has not yet been arrived at, and I must set forth my views on them somewhat more fully.

Historical and Philological Study of German is indispensable.

A true philologist is bound to investigate the language and literature of a nation in their historical development, or else he will be a mere *maître de langue*. As a rule, I have found that those who have objected most strongly to the historical study of German, and to the training of students in the philological (which is not merely an equivalent of 'grammatical') explanation of older German authors, themselves know nothing of Old German. The mere name of *Old High German*, and above all of *Gothic*, is enough to frighten them. While thus strongly objecting to the study of the older stages of German, they require a classical master to study the old Greek dialect of Homer, and are pleased if he has devoted some time to the study of dialects and inscriptions. They justly expect a botanist to know something of fossil plants, and rightly insist on a geologist knowing more than the mere surface of the earth. For the same very good reason, we maintain, no linguistic training, whether in an ancient or in a modern language, can be called scientific and thorough which is not largely historical. We want to trace and to show in the language the law of development, physiological and psychological. We want not merely to know but to understand.

By the aid of such study fossilized forms in modern German, typical phrases, apparent exceptions to general rules, become clear, and the close connection between German and English is forcibly brought out.

The history of the German language and literature, so far as we can trace it, covers a period of more than a thousand years, and shows us both in very different stages of development. Can we doubt that the study of the chief characteristics of each of these phases forms a most excellent schooling for the future teacher's mind? What can be more helpful for forming large views and a proper historical sense? What can afford the teacher a clearer insight into the real character and constitution of the German language and literature? We observe German speech while it remains still tolerably free from any foreign intellectual influence; we then perceive the gradual operation of the influence of Roman civilization; then that of the Christian Church makes itself strongly felt in language and literature; then we observe the influence of late Latin and early French and Italian civilization; the deep impression produced by the Crusades can be traced everywhere; now French medieval literature becomes of the greatest importance; the influence of the Renaissance and of the Reformation of the Church demands, and rewards, careful study; French and English culture, and the rapidly increasing intercourse between the great modern civilized nations—all these influences have left lasting traces in the language[1] no less than in the literature. Let me remind you of Paul Heyse's pretty 'Spruch':—

> 'Die Worte werden dir manches sagen,
> Verstehst du nur sie auszufragen.'

By the foregoing remarks I do not, however, intend to require a future teacher of German to give his chief attention to Old German or to Medieval literature. A schoolmaster only wants a sound knowledge of the principal facts of historical grammar; he wants a knowledge of the older periods of the language mainly in order to obtain through them a correct understanding of its modern form, a knowledge which saves him from making any of the annoying mistakes that are so often made by philologically untrained teachers.

If up to now I have only insisted on the importance of philological training on purely theoretical grounds, I now maintain that for practical reasons a good training in historical

[1] Compare Seiler's interesting book mentioned on p. 139.

grammar is of the greatest importance. A teacher may, at any moment, be called upon to give an explanation which he cannot give without some knowledge of older German or of historical grammar. He may also wish to have the clue to some interesting linguistic phenomena merely for his own satisfaction even if he is not called upon to explain it to his pupils. Questions, often of an apparently elementary nature, must crop up constantly in reading the great classics, or in discussing composition in the higher forms.

Let me give a few examples: Why do we say *Mond*, but *Monat*? *Wahn*, but *Argwohn*? Why *das Interesse* and *die Mätresse*? Shall we say *allesfalls* or *allenfalls*, *reines* or *reinen Herzens*? *Deutsch* or *teutsch*? *Meine edeln, teuern Freunde* or *edlen, teuren Freunde*? *feiern* or *feiren*? Is it right to say *bar Geld*, or should we say *bares Geld*? We always say: *auf gut Glück*. Is *verstünde* just as good as *verstände*, *däucht* as *dünkt*, *hub* as *hob*, *fodern* as *fordern*, *empfahn* as *empfangen*? How are *hangen*, *hängen* and *henken* used in older and in Modern German? Would you allow pupils to say *der Rock hangt am Nagel* or *da hangen drei Hüte*? Why is it *der Henker*? Ought one to write *er frug* or *er fragte*? *er ladete* or *er lud*? Does it matter which is used? How would you explain lines in well-known poems of Goethe, Uhland and Dach, such as: *Die Augen täten ihm sinken*; *die Stätt, wo Roland jüngst gestritten hätt'*; *der wackre Schwabe forcht', sich nit*; *käm' alles Wetter gleich auf uns zu schlahn*? Why do we say *hoch* —*höher*; *näher*—*nächst*; *rauh*—*Rauchwerk*? *rechnen* but *Rechenbuch*; *zeichnen* but *Zeichenlehrer*? Why *Majestät*? Ought a teacher of German to be ignorant of the reasons why it is *er nimmt*, but *sie nehmen*; *wenden*, *wandte*, but *blenden*, *blendete*; *denken*, *dachte*, but *senken*, *senkte*; *gehe*, *ging*, but *stehe*, *stand*, *sehe*, *sah*, *wehe*, *wehte*? Is it correct to say that *wandte* is 'of the mixed conjugation'? Why is it *er beißt*, but *er weiß*? what is *er weißt*? *er macht*, but *er mag*; *er gönnt*, but *er kann*? What is the history of the forms of address? *Er, Sie, Ihr* (all of which are found in 'Hermann und Dorothea'), and of *begonnte* riming with *konnte*? How would he account for the plurals *Mann, Männer, Mannen*; *Lande, Länder*; *Orte, Örter*; *Worte, Wörter*; or for the reasons for the different gender in *der Heide* and *die Heide, der Tor* and *das Tor*? or for the composition of *Mondlicht, Mondenschein, Mondesglanz*; *Frauenkirche, Frauentor, Frauenzimmer*? What is *die Moderne*? How would you explain its formation? Explain : *über See*, but *übers Meer fahren*; *im Himmel und auf Erden*. Explain: *der Schurz, die Schürze*; *der* and *das Gemahl*; *das Waffen* and *die Waffe*; '*Christ ist erstanden*,' but *kein Christenmensch*; *er blieb stehen*; *der zu schreibende Brief*; *es* (and *das*) *nimmt mich wunder*; *hier ist seines Bleibens nicht*; *saget niemand nichts*; *er nimmt an nichts keinen Anteil*; *keinen wirklichen Nebel sahe Achilles nicht*; *Gott schuf den Menschen ihm zum Bilde*; *der Sohn, so ihm der Herr gegeben*; *ich bin ein guter Hirte*; *an ein hohes Ministerium*; *es fiel ein Reif in der Frühlingsnacht*; *ich weiß mir ein schönes Jungfräulein*; *was da der edeln Garben auf allen Feldern lag*; *er küßte sie an den Mund so bleich*; *nun bin ich wie andre Ritter wert*; etc. An acquaintance with older German is also indispensable for the right explanation of nouns such as *Bursch* (*Es zogen drei Bursche wohl über den Rhein*), *Knabe* (*Jung Siegfried war ein stolzer Knab*), *Fräulein* (*Bin weder Fräulein weder schön*), *Tugend* (*ich messe mich mit Euch in jeder ritterlichen Tugend*), *meinen* (in *Freiheit, die ich meine*), *Lieb* (*zu liebe tun, Lieb und Leid*), *Schimpf* (in *Schimpf und Ernst*), *Rat* (*Gerät, Hausrat*, etc.), *Wonne* (in *Wonnemonat*), *Haupt* and *Kopf, Minne* and *Liebe*, etc., or of common adjectives such as *stolz, mild, frech, fromm, frei, keck, reich, siech, hell* (in *in hellen Haufen*), *schlecht* (in *schlecht und recht*), and others.

Again, it is most instructive to compare German and English—within proper limits. Some knowledge of older English, including Chaucer's 'Canterbury Tales,' is, no doubt, possessed by most Modern Language teachers. Why, then, is it, that if in a great many cases English *o* (*oa*) corresponds to German *ei* (e.g. home, stone, bone, alone, soap, broad, etc.), we find in several strong preterites English *o* corresponding to German *i* (rode, smote, wrote, etc.)? Or again, if German *t* corresponds as a rule to English *d* (*tot, Brot, Not, rot*, etc.), how is it that *wert* corresponds to *worth*? The slightest knowledge of M.H.G. explains in both cases the apparent anomaly[1].

Teachers should have definite views, based on scientific principles, on important everyday questions concerning their subject, e.g. the much discussed question of spelling reform (German, French, English). How far is reform still needed or desirable in Germany since the changes of 1902? How far is a spelling reform practicable? Should we continue to represent the same sound by different symbols, e.g. *f, v, ph, pph; i, y; i, ih, ie; ei, ai,* and what is the historical difference between the symbols for the same sound? Should reformers adopt the historical or the phonetic principle, or a mixture of the two? What attempts have been made in Germany up to the present time? Is it desirable to have an academy regulating the spelling from time to time? Is there at present in Germany any Society the authority and functions of which can be compared with those of the *Académie Française*? What are the aims and what is the influence of the *Allgemeiner deutscher Sprachverein*? Ought an English teacher of German to support it? To what extent should capital letters be employed? When and in what way were they first introduced into German writing and printing? Should we teach the use of Latin or of German letters? Are the so-called Gothic letters a national *cachet* and a valuable characteristic of the German language? How did the *u* hook and the modification marks arise? How did *h* come to be used as a symbol denoting length of a vowel? Why is long *i* often rendered by *ie*? What is the best German pronunciation? Is it

---

[1] See my Pitt Press edition of 'Doctor Wespe' by R. Benedix ([2]1895), where, at the end of the notes, 'Rules for Etymological Comparison' of the German and English sounds are given which will prove useful to teachers.

Hanoverian German? If an older pupil is sent abroad for one or two months, does it much matter if he goes to Dresden or to Bremen, to Bochum or to Stuttgart? To what extent does an ordinary German New Testament, as sold by the Bible Societies, represent the linguistic form of Dr Luther's New Testament? Are the differences at all important? Cheap specimens of the original Luther texts are published in the 'Sammlung Goeschen,' and in Dr Reifferscheid's useful edition of the 'Marcus Evangelion Mart. Luther's nach der Septemberbibel' (Heilbronn, 1889). Teachers should have thought about all these things during their academical course, and should have worked out these and similar questions for themselves under the guidance of the University professor.

Why should a Teacher of MODERN *German know some* OLD *High German?*

There are many people who, while fully admitting the necessity of a future teacher being trained in historical grammar, yet suppose a knowledge of Middle High German to be sufficient for the purpose. Correspondences, such as *I rode —ich ritt*, are easily explained by M.H.G., and so are, in fact, many of the more elementary questions of historical grammar. Is, then, M.H.G. not really sufficient for the wants of a teacher? I have been asked this question more than once; allow me to answer it once more in this connection. I thoroughly believe some knowledge of O.H.G. to be indispensable to a future teacher of German. My reasons are the following: Firstly, O.H.G. is essential on account of the preservation of the full vowels in unaccented syllables, which were in M.H.G. all weakened into *e*. Thus only in O.H.G. we have the clue to the explanation of vowel mutation (*Umlaut*), e.g. *scōni* > *schön*, *scōno* > *schon*; *handin* (later *hendin*), *handun* > *Händen*, *vor-handen*. (For the explanation of *handun* some Gothic is welcome.) The modern change in the radical vowels of words, such as *Erde, irden*; *sehen, sieht*; *nehmen, nimmt*; *Gold, gülden*; *bieten, beut*; *wurden, würden*, can only be satisfactorily explained by the O.H.G. forms *erda, irdīn*; *sehan, sihit*; *neman, nimit*; *gold, guldīn*; *biotan, biutit*; *wurdun, wurdin*. In O.H.G. many of the later contractions had not yet taken place. The modern and M.H.G. *Mensch* is still *mannisco*, our *welsch* is *walhisc*, our *Amt* (M.H.G. *ambet*) is *ambaht, glauben* is *gilouban, bleiben* is *bilîban, Menge* is *managi, welch* is *huuelîh, Rabe* is *hraban, Roß* is *hros, Nuß* is *hnuz, laut* is *hlût*, etc. A knowledge of O.H.G. consonants is needed for a full scientific understanding of the laws of sound-shifting, and analogous cases might be given from other parts of grammar. Even some elementary Gothic is sometimes help ful, e.g. in explaining such preterites as *er hieß*, from *hiez, hiaz, hēz, hēt*, **hĕh·t, hĕhait* (Gothic spelling: *haíhait*), or *ließ*, from *liez, liaz, lēz, lēt*, **lĕl·t, lĕlōt* (Gothic *laílot*); the O.H.G. reduplicated form *teta* ('I or he did') immediately explains the indicative *täte* in Uhland's *Da täten sie sich trennen*, or Goethe's *Des täten die Musen sich erfreun*. The reduplication in Latin and Greek suggests itself for comparison.

Again, if the student wishes to form a correct idea of the oldest German versification—i.e. the style of alliterative poetry—he will find some scanty fragments of it preserved in O.H.G. alone, while in later German only isolated alliterative phrases (*singen und sagen, Leib und Leben, Kind und Kegel, Mann und Maus, Stock und Stein, Wind und Wetter, dichten und trachten*, for older *tichten und trachten*, etc.) survive.

I should therefore advise every future teacher of Modern German to read some representative O.H.G., M.H.G., and sixteenth century classics. He should have read them in order to study the language in connected texts. He should not, like many students of comparative philology, study isolated words. He must examine sentences, explain idiomatic expressions, investigate peculiarities of style (in prose and poetry), appreciate the metre, in short, enter fully into the spirit of the language at different periods, but at the same time not lose sight of the fact that it is not for the sake of the language only that he ought to study the old classics.

For these reasons I insist on my pupils reading a sufficient, though not excessive, amount of Older German. I know from a long experience that most of those who care for the study, and other students should not be encouraged to become teachers of Modern Languages, do this willingly. I am personally quite free from any undue predilection for medievalism, but I am concerned that all parts of my subject should receive the attention which is due to them. While taking a great deal of interest in Old German authors, I certainly consider Modern German literature, on the whole, to be much superior to the Old, quite apart from its greater practical importance, and consequently deserving of much closer study. But it cannot be seriously questioned that a good foundation in the philological study of any modern language should be laid at the University— the only place where it can be laid satisfactorily—otherwise it must be left to the energy of the individual teacher to acquire a sufficient amount of the necessary information by private reading. To obtain this information by his own unaided efforts is .a very difficult task. It is much easier to make oneself more proficient in the modern language and literature after the University course is finished. A young graduate can continue his training in modern literature by means of residence abroad and by private study. See pages 107—112.

There seems to be much less doubt as to the training which a teacher of German wants with regard to the modern language. It is agreed on all sides that he should, (*a*) pronounce German words correctly, and the sentences with proper intonation; (*b*) secondly, that he should find his words easily, choose them fitly, master the principal synonyms, etc.; and (*c*) thirdly, that he should construct his phrases not only correctly, but idiomatically.

Pronunciation.

I think the very great practical importance of *pronunciation* is not yet sufficiently insisted on in all quarters, and the high value of *phonetic* training is recognised still less.

A teacher should possess a correct pronunciation, and a sufficient knowledge of the auxiliary science of phonetics, to be able to teach the conscious imitation of foreign sounds.

He must show his pupils that sounds which are usually considered to be the same are by no means pronounced exactly alike in German and English. He will point out the difference between apparently similar groups of sounds, such as the English *fear* and German *vier*; he will not allow his boys to pronounce the German *rot* like the English *wrote*, *Koffer* like (*s*)*coffer*, or *Lehm* like *lame*, as they are told in some books to do. He will inform them of the different values of *r*, or *s*, or *sch* (*sh*), or *l*, etc., in the two languages. See pages 18—19 and 69 sqq.

Every mistake of the master will be magnified by his boys. The acquisition of a good and idiomatic pronunciation should therefore be from the first lesson an object of constant effort. Dictation given by a teacher with a strong Saxon pronunciation will make the boys write *Freide*, *umhillen*, etc. No difference will be made between *gefreut* and *gefreit*, *gönnen* and *kennen*. The mistakes which a modern language master makes in pronunciation are much more serious than those of his classical colleague. It is certainly by no means unimportant how we pronounce *pater peccavi* or *vicissim*, but we cannot, under any circumstances, allow the boys to say: *swonsig*, *Nacht* (with palatal *ch*), *Göld*, *Fin-ger*, *Boseuuikt*, *fumf*. A criminal who is *geächtet* (outlawed) should not be called *geachtet* (esteemed). A tournament is fought *in den Schranken* and not *in den Schränken*, and a pretty girl should not be called *ein hubsches Madchen*. It seems strange that this important part of a teacher's training should not have received full recognition till comparatively recently.   Scholars who shudder at the slightest grammatical blunder, e.g. the use of a wrong gender, a wrong case, or a wrong preposition, and who severely censure the smallest mistake made in the recognised spelling of a word, do not mind (or notice) a very bad pronunciation, which would grate on a native's ear.

The important question: What is correct German, and where should German pronunciation be studied? has been discussed on pages 66 and following.

Importance of Training in Phonetics.

The scientific study of phonetics should be left to the University training, but a rough classification of sounds may well be given at school, and the fundamental axioms of phonetics, e.g. 'a (spoken) word consists of sounds and *not* of letters' (cp. *Scherz*: *Sch* = 1 sound, *z* = 2 sounds, viz. *t* + *s*), should be impressed on the boys and girls as early as possible.

At the University the training must become more full and systematic. The student must be trained, and train himself, to observe and to imitate consciously. He should learn to analyse the sounds of a foreign idiom, and to compare them with those of his native tongue. He must know the special difficulties which German offers to English students, in order to help his class to overcome them. Such marked provincialisms as the Westphalian *Schinken* (*sχiŋkən*), the Swabian *Geischt, Oberscht, re(a)cht* (with guttural *ch*), the Berlin *janz und jar, Biene* instead of *Bühne, Mutta*, the Bavarian *Moasta* (=*Meister*), the Saxon inability to distinguish between *treu* and *drei, Röte* and *Rede, Türe* and *Tiere, Ende* and *Ente, Orden* and *Orten, Greis* and *Kreis, Bein* and *Pein* will be studied scientifically. He should also know what the pronunciation of Schiller and Goethe was like and to what extent it is reflected in their poetry.

On the other hand, the importance of phonetics should not be overrated; a teacher need not be a phonetic specialist. He has other and more important subjects to study; his time of preparation is too short. Phonetics must be for him merely a subsidiary subject. The chief thing for the great majority of school-children will always be to learn to read the foreign language with ease, to read much, and to enjoy the treasures of foreign literature.

This is what I believe a higher or specialist teacher of German should know. Now the question arises: What kind of training will enable him to put himself in possession of the above-mentioned qualifications? I am aware of the fact that up to now many excellent teachers of German—Englishmen or Germans—have, for one reason or another, not gone through a course such as I am recommending. Their way must have been all the more beset with difficulties, and our appreciation of their energy and talents will of necessity be all the greater. But the growing interest in the study of modern languages, and the increasing provision for it made by our Universities have now given many encouragements and facilities which it would be wrong for intending students to ignore.

I shall, in what follows, distinguish between the training obtainable in Great Britain and the training which should be gone through abroad.

The *training in Great Britain* may be considered under three heads, viz.:—

(*a*) Firstly, the *preparatory training at school.*

(*b*) Secondly, the *University curriculum.* (Three, and if possible four, years of higher study.)

(*c*) Thirdly, the self-training of the teacher at a school.

TRAINING IN GREAT BRITAIN.

(*a*) *At School.*

I should like to make a few remarks under this head, as possibly some masters preparing boys for the study of modern languages may care to consider them.

A boy who wishes to become a teacher of modern languages *should not specialize too early*, but should endeavour to become as proficient as possible in languages, ancient as well as modern, and also in history and geography. I much regret the hard and fast line which is usually drawn between classical and modern languages. A future teacher of modern languages should be most anxious to know something of the two ancient languages and literatures ; such knowledge cannot fail to be of great interest and advantage to him[1]. He will get in this way a good general linguistic training ; he will learn many characteristics of the classical languages, which will be of great value to him in studying modern languages ; many words will be learnt which will be useful for philological comparisons. A boy who has read classics is, to some extent, familiar with the chief classical metres, a knowledge of which is indispensable for the study of modern German poets, such as Klopstock, Goethe, Hölderlin, Platen, Geibel, etc. Ancient literature has exercised a great influence on German and other modern literatures, which cannot be justly appreciated by a man destitute of classical knowledge. Many of Goethe's masterpieces were composed under the direct influence of classical models.

For these reasons I should strongly advise a boy who wishes to study modern languages not to neglect at school the study of the classics, and to learn more than the bare minimum required in order to enable him to pass the University Entrance Examinations; nothing can afford a future language teacher a better preparation than a connected study of the ancient and modern languages, together with the elements of universal history and the main facts of European geography.

He should also be especially proficient in the mother-tongue. He should have had careful training in writing English; he should know how to arrange and connect his thoughts ; he should have had years of practice in essay-writing, as school-boys get it in Germany and in France.

[1] See my pamphlet on 'Greek and its humanistic alternatives in the Little-go,' Cambridge, 1905, pages 4 and 18.

With regard to the *special* school training in German, the following seems to be essential. First of all, a boy must acquire a good pronunciation. He should have, as early as possible, regular practice in speaking, his master making it a point to talk German to his classes almost from the beginning during some part of the lesson; he should recite (and in some cases sing) first little popular rimes and songs, later on poems, prose fables, striking passages from speeches, etc.; he should learn to open his mouth, to use his lips, to articulate clearly and distinctly, and in every way to overcome his natural shyness in speaking and imitating foreign sounds. In the middle forms he should begin to write original German, which is really easier than translation from English into German. Little descriptions or reproductions of a story afford good practice at the beginning; simple letters might follow; a natural gradation of subjects should be devised; he should regularly write from dictation; he should not learn any Old German or receive any systematic instruction in historical grammar. But in a boy who wishes to become a teacher of languages the sense of historical development should be aroused early; he should have some notion of the real meaning of 'rules' and 'exceptions'; he might be expected to have some idea of *mots populaires* and *mots savants* in French (*meuble* and *mobile*), or, in German, have a notion of the existence of different groups of loan words coming from the same source, e.g. *Kerker* and *Karzer*; *Orgel* and *Organ*; *Pfaffe, Papst, Papa, Pope*, etc. He should have a correct and clear conception of the principal facts of sound-shifting (but not merely write confusedly about '*W*erner's Law'!), e.g.

d e a d	d ea th	(shep)herd	hearth	t en	m a k e
t o t	t o d	Hirt	Herd	z e h n	m a ch en

give	p o u n d	p i p e	d r o p	
g e b en	Pf u n d	Pf ei f e	Tr o pf en	etc.

These should suffice. An advanced boy might, before coming

up to the University, read some little book on German, such as Wasserzieher's two little pamphlets 'Aus dem Leben der deutschen Sprache' (3*d.* each) in 'Wissenschaftliche Volksbibliothek,' Nos. 14 and 78. But he should not go too far, and should be especially careful about the use of philological terms.

If a boy wants to compete for a scholarship, he might use Brandt's 'German Grammar' in addition to his school grammar, and read through a number of well-annotated editions of modern classics. If he wishes to begin the study of M.H.G. between his school and his University course, he should not follow the usual guessing method, but should use Zupitza's practical and reliable 'Einführung in das Studium des M.H.D.,' and read through one or two of the nice little volumes of the 'Sammlung Göschen.' But, above all, he should be well trained—as far as can reasonably be expected of a boy—in understanding, speaking, reading, and writing Modern German ; he should be able to do a piece of easy composition creditably, and have some practice in writing a simple original composition in idiomatic style. In order to make himself proficient in this he might be advised before coming up to the University to spend four to six months abroad in a suitable family.

It is most important that boys should come to the University with a good start of general information, and also reasonably well grounded in their special subject. They have, as a rule, only three years at their disposal, and the terms are very short ; while in Germany most men find it now necessary to devote four years to their studies. Intending students should at once consult the University professors and lecturers about their work. In one respect it is essentially different from that of all other students ; it cannot be well carried out in Great Britain alone. A parent allowing his son to study modern languages should be prepared to let him go abroad, at least once or twice in the vacations. The omission of such foreign training would be a great loss to his son. To him foreign countries are what laboratories are to the student of science.

All indications point to a great future for properly trained modern language students, men and women, but we want bright students for the work, not such as cannot do anything else, and only rely on their having lived abroad for some time. They should not take up Modern Languages because they think the study of them easier than that of anything else; but because they care for the subject, and are anxious to know more of the language, literature, culture, and spirit of some of the most important nations of the world. They will some day, as teachers, be called upon to interpret foreign ideas to their own countrymen, to promote at home a just appreciation of foreign excellence. The minds of the next generation are to be formed partly by them; their task is as noble as it is responsible. Idle boys without ideas or ideals, who have merely resided abroad for some time, will never perform that task.

A student who comes to the University, intending to read for an Honours course in Modern Languages, should have completed his reading for his Preliminary Examinations, so that he can devote at least three clear years to his special study. This is too often neglected, and the loss of time cannot, under the present system, be made up. If he is not ready to pass his Entrance Examination at once, let him defer coming up for a year, and spend, if possible, a few months abroad in carefully chosen surroundings.

(b) University Training.

The University course stands in the centre of a modern language master's training. The student gets here, better than he gets it from any books, a general and methodical survey of the whole domain of his subject. He will, later on, till but a limited field himself, but he should not start as a narrow specialist. He should be early accustomed to look over the fences and hedges, and see what place his work must take in the cultivation of the whole land. Perhaps he may some day single out a favourite and promising spot where he will dig deep. A science which is as young as ours requires frequent explanation and discussion by the professor. Here the student learns to think about his subject, he is initiated into *methodical work*; he learns to view the development of language and literature in the light of history; he learns not only the facts, but their inner connection; he becomes acquainted with the critical interpretation of old and modern texts. Moreover much of a modern language student's work cannot be done by himself in the study. It must be done in the lecture room.

At our Universities we teach much more than a master either can or should directly use in class; but a good schoolmaster ought to be widely read in his subject. How else can he make a suitable choice of the books to be used, or decide about methods to be adopted? He must also know by experience how scientific results in his subject are obtained, or how far certain current linguistic or literary theories can be considered as well established. He ought not to be dependent on the language and literature primers which he happens to find in use at the school in which he teaches. This thorough information about his subject is the indispensable background for every single piece of his work; it is the shadow which he casts—to borrow a suggestive simile from Chamisso's 'Peter Schlemihl'—and without which, although he cannot use it directly, he will everywhere feel hampered and embarrassed.

The University cannot and should not be expected to train students of modern languages exclusively for the profession of teacher. The University has a twofold aim, viz. :— (*a*) to promote science (*die Wissenschaft*), and to train scholars for that purpose; (*b*) secondly, to prepare men qualified to do good work in different branches of practical life, which means, in our case, (1) teachers, (2) writers and critics, (3) librarians, (4) diplomatists, (5) civil servants, (6) men of business. We have had students reading for all these different professions; the University course should be so arranged as to benefit all these different classes. It would be a serious mistake to neglect the wants of the scholar; it must be our aim to establish at the British Universities a *thoroughly good British modern languages school*, producing valuable work. It is true that a large percentage of men and women come up with a view to becoming teachers; but I believe that the Universities, without professing to prepare them for their task more than other students, nevertheless do this as a matter of fact, and that he or she who knows how to profit by the instruction can secure an excellent training. A student should only beware of imagining that the University can do everything for him. Much must be left to his own individual efforts, and the end of the University course does not at all imply that his training as a teacher has come to an end. He should go on working and improving his knowledge no less than his practical experience.

The chief subjects of University study are: (1) Firstly, the advanced study of the language, including oral drill, phonetics, essays, the history of the language, and the study of specimens of the German language in old and modern times. (2) Secondly, the study of literature, including representative authors from the various periods, the history of German, and comparison with English, literature, the theory of metre, and the theory of poetry. (3) Thirdly, 'realia,' i.e. the outlines of German life and thought, customs, institutions, and general conditions of life in old and modern times.

To master even the chief facts of all these subjects is no small matter, and requires at least three clear years of conscientious work. Provision is made in the Cambridge Tripos that a student may stay on for a fourth year, and take up, if he likes, one of the more strictly philological sections, or read for one of the English sections in connection with his modern language work, unless he prefers to stay a fourth year without taking any other examination, solely with the view of extending his knowledge and, if possible, doing a certain amount of original work.

The student should attend all the University lectures by which he is likely to profit, and not be discouraged if, at first, he should fail to understand every word of those delivered in the foreign language. The ear naturally requires considerable training, but I know from experience that, after some time, he will be able to follow with ease. He should take good lecture notes, and read them over and correct them, or make abstracts of them where necessary, soon after the lecture. He should add to them by later reading. Good notes are especially important in modern languages, because the subject is so new. Many printed books on philology and historical grammar are obsolescent or superseded; new theories are crowding in from everywhere; the teacher's part is thus particularly important, and it would be indeed humiliating if it could be said of a University lecturer on modern languages:—

'Dass er nichts sagt, als was im Buche steht.'

The exercises in speaking and writing should never, during the whole course, be interrupted; original composition, especially, should not be neglected. The ear should also be trained by dictation, and the speech organs practised by frequent recitation. Poems and prose pieces of striking excellence should be learned by heart, and often repeated; philological and literary exercises should not be neglected, and, in an advanced class, students should be trained in the methodical explanation of texts, and in criticism. Such students as wish for private tuition, in addition to University and College teaching, should, if possible, seek scientific instruction through the medium of the foreign language. The private work of the student should be partly scientific, partly practical. He ought to read up the prescribed subjects and, as far as he can, the great masterpieces of modern literature. He should work carefully through his lecture notes, alone or with a fellow-student. He should make it a point to go frequently to the University library or to a Modern Language Students' library to read up references to books and scientific periodicals. The practical work includes wide reading of representative German of our own time, and the study of the best magazines and newspapers, or of well written novels, representing German life and thought.

If the work during the term is chiefly scientific, the vacation work will be chiefly modern and literary.

A student who is not obliged to spend the whole vacation at home, or part of it at a British University, may very profitably spend some months on the Continent, in a town where he can see some of the great classical plays which he is studying acted on the stage. Indeed it is highly desirable that students should, *as a matter of course*, arrange to spend some of their vacations, especially the two long vacations, on the Continent,— in those countries the languages of which they are studying. At most British Universities there are opportunities of conversing with natives of Germany and France. Students should try to profit by them. If there is a Modern Language Club, the student should join it. Many men have been abroad at different places; an exchange of experience and impressions must be of value for all members. The student should also try to get to know the professor or University lecturer in his subject and obtain his advice when in doubt or difficulty. I shall discuss the study of 'realia' in connection with the training abroad.

(c) *Training after the University Course, Self-Training.*

A student who has qualified in the highest University examinations can safely be left to himself, but he will probably realize that, if he wants to become a successful school teacher of German, his training is not yet finished. Apart from the necessary methical study of the art of teaching and of its auxiliary subjects, ethics and psychology, and apart from storing up practical experience gained by school teaching and by hearing lessons given by good practical teachers, he will go on studying the classical and many representative modern authors, reading foreign periodicals and magazines, scientific and literary, and also good newspapers, collecting cuttings of particularly good articles. He may subscribe to one or two, such as *Die Neueren Sprachen*, the *Archiv für das Studium der Neueren Sprachen und Litteraturen*, and a magazine, such as *Die Woche*, *Das literarische Echo*, or the *Deutsche Rundschau*. In reading German he should use Heyne's, Paul's, or Weigand's dictionaries (latest editions), in which the words are explained in German. He should endeavour to keep up regular intercourse with natives, for which there are many opportunities in large towns, especially in London. He might exchange lessons or conversation, or even correspondence. No less should he cultivate the society of teachers of modern languages. By joining the 'Modern Language Association' he would come into contact with other modern language masters, and would have excellent opportunities of exchanging experience. He should now turn earnestly to the study of books on method, and test promising theories by his practical experience. At the University, before he had completed his degree course, there was little time for such studies, but now is the right time for them.

Realia.

The adherents of the 'new method' have rightly insisted that in the training of modern language masters greater prominence should be given to the study of those auxiliary subjects, without some knowledge of which a master would not be fully qualified for his work. As I have said before, the life and thought of the nation, the outlines of its institutions and customs, social relations, history and geography, philosophy and religion, are comprised in this general term. An English teacher of German should be especially well informed about

German school and University life. In teaching he might use picture post-cards, limelight views and perhaps—in ten or fifteen years' time,—a good cinematograph. He might possibly make use of a combination of the phonograph and cinematograph.

For general information and reference to larger works, nothing can be better than Meyer's handy 'Kleines Konversations Lexikon,' or 'Der Kleine Brockhaus.' See pages 158—9. For history and geography, the teacher will do well to buy the best current German and French school books.

TRAINING ABROAD.

We have seen that, however successfully a student and young master may work in Great Britain, a most essential part of his training must be gone through on the Continent. Large schools, Universities, County Councils, private donors should all help modern language students and teachers in obtaining this very necessary training abroad[1]. A student should, however, take good care to arrive on the Continent well prepared, or else the stay abroad will profit him but little. The importance of the place selected is too much underrated by Professor Bréal in his suggestive book *De l'enseignement des langues vivantes* (pp. 40—1). A *North* German town is certainly to be preferred to a South or Middle German one, a large town to a small town ; a University town offers many additional advantages ; the capital of a country should be known to a teacher in the first instance. Berlin or Paris should consequently be chosen by preference. When they are well known to the student, and after a good pronunciation has been acquired, he may reside for some time in a small and pretty Middle or South German place, e.g. at Weimar (near Jena and Eisenach) or Marburg, or at Heidelberg

[1] For travelling bursaries, posts of assistants at Prussian state schools, etc. see pages 38 sqq. and 170—1.

or Freiburg. There is a great difference between North and South German speech, life, and character, and a teacher should know and appreciate both. The decentralization of Germany is as interesting as it is fortunate[1].

About the length of the stay abroad no definite rule can be laid down. Of course, the longer the better; but the student should, at least, have passed one whole long vacation in Germany, and a teacher should make it a point to go again, from time to time, so as not to get rusty. The best plan for a future German master is to arrange to spend at least six months in Germany immediately after having taken his degree. Only then may he hope to become well acquainted with Germany and the Germans. Especially should a teacher beware of rash generalizations, and not say, after a very short stay in one place, 'I know Germany[2].' A student should stay with a refined German family, and should avoid all boarding-houses announcing 'English comfort,' 'afternoon tea,' etc. He should expressly stipulate that he should be the only foreigner received at that time. The family of a German secondary teacher will be, for obvious reasons, the best for him to go to. University professors do not, as a rule, take boarders. English teachers of limited means may sometimes reduce

[1] If students or teachers can manage to go more than once, they should make it a point to see different parts of the country.

[2] With regard to France, a student and teacher of French will do well to go to the capital and study the French language and French literature, life and institutions there. He can now obtain excellent advice and guidance in the 'Institut Français pour étrangers,' in the 'École des Hautes Études Sociales,' 16 Rue de la Sorbonne, which has recently been opened under the able directorship of Dr Schweitzer, the well-known French professor and educationist. The foundation of this 'Institut' is largely due to the suggestions made by me in 1900 in my pamphlet 'Betrachtungen und Vorschläge betreffend die Gründung eines Reichsinstituts für Lehrer des Englischen in London,' Leipzig, Stolte, 1900, and in my speech at the Neuphilologentag at Breslau (1902), 'Mittel und Wege zur Beförderung der praktischen Ausbildung unserer neusprachlichen Lehrer' (printed in the 'Verhandlungen des x. deutschen Neuphilologentages,' pp. 65 sqq.).

expenses by giving or exchanging lessons, but one who is not thus obliged to reduce his expenses should not sacrifice part of his valuable time abroad to work which does not materially promote his own training. Teachers who have been abroad before may like to join some of the numerous Modern Language Holiday Courses[1].

Once settled in a foreign country, a student should hear, see, and speak as much as possible; he should attend public lectures, University lectures, hear sermons and political debates; he should make German acquaintances, know students and teachers, walk, talk, and read with them. I usually tell my students: First of all speak much in the family with which you stay, and insist on having your pronunciation corrected; keep studiously away from everything English; live with Germans in the German way, even if you do not like everything at first; try to be introduced into *good* German society, and study society life; join in a *Schulreise*, witness a great public festival, a *Turnfest, Schulfest, Sängerfest*; a military display; attend the meetings of a *Philologentag* or *Künstlerverein* or *Liedertafel*; go to the theatres, and read the plays beforehand; buy and analyse different German newspapers and magazines, subscribe to a lending library; analyse and discuss with your German friends and teachers such books as Mrs Sidgwick's 'Home life in Germany,' S. Whitman's 'Imperial Germany,' Dawson's 'German life in town and country,' or novels such as Mrs Sidgwick's 'The Professor's legacy,' or Ompteda's 'Heimat des Herzens,' and others. Try to be admitted to the University library, and, if you happen to be at Heidelberg, see not only the great tun but the great Minnesinger manuscript; see the great works of art, and endeavour to find out which subjects are best treated and which are treated by preference; compare the North and South German comic papers, and compare them with the Austrian, French, and English—you will find that all have an individuality of

[1] See page 41.

their own; take lessons in original composition from interesting native teachers, describe your impressions, and ask your teacher and your friends about everything that strikes you; take, if possible, some lessons on pronunciation and delivery of classical poetry and prose passages from a good actor or actress; keep a diary in which you enter anything that strikes you as characteristic of foreign life together with any explanation that may have been given by your German friends and teachers; collect illustrated catalogues and large railway maps and prospectuses (containing views of the Rhine, the Black Forest railway, the Lake of Lucerne, etc.) which you can easily obtain abroad at railway stations and information bureaus; buy photographs[1] and picture post-cards, e.g. Heidelberg Castle, Cologne Cathedral, Nürnberg churches, the Wartburg, the Roland of Bremen and Halle, Bismarck at Hamburg and Berlin, Lübeck gates, the old Coronation halls of Aachen and Frankfurt, the Goethe-Schiller Monument at Weimar, etc. Procure some collection of popular songs with music, and books illustrating German life, customs, and popular costumes in different parts of the Empire, Austria, and Switzerland; buy a good school atlas—you will want detailed maps of Germany with the German names; read and collect German books written in a truly German spirit, not the poor imitators of Zola and Ibsen whose work will soon be forgotten; form the nucleus of a serviceable private library, there being many ways of getting good modern literature at very cheap prices[2]. Finally,

---

[1] A good series is the one mentioned on p. 160 note.

[2] For dramatic literature there are 'Die Meisterwerke der deutschen Bühne,' edited (with helpful introductions) by G. Witkowski. For other cheap series of lyrics and novels, see pages 150—1. Some modern books, novels and plays, are also procurable abroad at very reasonable prices in good second-hand copies, catalogues of which can be obtained free of charge from German booksellers. Teachers should also collect some first-rate illustrations of German classics, such as W. von Kaulbach's 'Goethe-Gallerie' (with Friedrich Spielhagen's text) and similar works of art.

try to be admitted to good schools, and attend lessons in modern languages, the mother-tongue, and history in different classes.

This is what I wished to say concerning the training of modern language masters. You will have noticed that a training such as I propose for intending teachers of modern languages is just as long, and their work at least as hard, as sound, as important and dignified, as that of their classical colleagues. They have to master one, or even two, exceedingly difficult languages, to be acquainted with the masterpieces of a rich literature extending over many centuries; they have not only to write, but to *speak*, these languages easily and with genuine foreign intonation. This requires them to go through a special scientific and practical training of the ear and of the speech organs, and involves expensive stays abroad.

To bring about an improvement in the status of duly qualified modern language masters is one of the principal aims of the Modern Language Association[1], of which I most heartily approve.

---

[1] Information about the aims of the Association, list of members, publications, etc. can be obtained from the Hon. Secretary, G. F. Bridge, Esq., 45 South Hill Park, Hampstead, London, N.W. The minimum annual subscription will in future be 7s. 6d. instead of 10s. 6d., and members who join after September 1st in any year will pay one subscription of 8s. 6d. for the remainder of that year and the following year. The subscription will entitle members to receive *Modern Language Teaching* post free, but not the *Modern Language Review*. They may, however, purchase the latter Journal for 7s. 6d. per annum instead of the published price of 12s. 6d. See p. 114.

BIBLIOGRAPHICAL APPENDIX

PERIODICALS[1].

1. *The Modern Language Quarterly* (for some years, *The Modern Quarterly of Language and Literature*). Edited by H. Frank Heath, with the assistance of E. G. W. Braunholtz, Karl Breul, I. Gollancz, E. L. Milner-Barry, A. W. Pollard, W. Rippmann, and V. Spiers. London. Seven volumes 1897—1904. (2s. 6d. each part.) Quarterly. Now split up into two separate publications :—

2. *The Modern Language Review.* Quarterly. Edited (with the assistance of an advisory board of leading English scholars) by John G. Robertson. Cambridge. University Press. Since October, 1905. It appears four times a year and costs 12s. 6d. net post free per annum, single numbers 4s. net. But see p. 113 note. This is the strictly scholarly portion.

3. *Modern Language Teaching.* Monthly. Edited (with the assistance of an advisory committee of secondary teachers) by Walter Rippmann. London. Black. Since March, 1905. Yearly eight numbers. (6d. a number.)

4. *The School World.* Often contains good articles, sometimes especially devoted to modern languages, e.g March, 1901 (Vol. III. no. 27. Special number). (6d. a number.)

5. *Modern Language Notes.* Edited by A. Marshall Elliott, James W. Bright, Hans C. G. v. Jagemann, Henry Alfred Todd. Baltimore. Since 1886. Eight numbers a year. (Subscription in advance, 7s. a year[2].)

[1] The full titles of most of the previously mentioned and of many other important periodicals are given in the first chapter of my *Handy Guide.* The *Journal of Education* and *The School World* should also be referred to and consulted throughout.

[2] A number of American Periodicals, also Transactions and Proceedings of American Modern Language Associations, are not included as unfortunately they can hardly be anywhere consulted in this country. But see Reports 4 and 5.

6. *Archiv für das Studium der Neueren Sprachen und Littera-turen.* Started by Ludwig Herrig. Braunschweig. Since 1846. Continued by Julius Zupitza and Adolf Tobler. Now edited (since 1903, Vol. 111) by Aloys Brandl and Heinrich Morf. The 121st volume has just been finished. Braunschweig. 1908–9. Half-yearly. (8s. per volume.)

7. *Die Neueren Sprachen*, Zeitschrift für den Neusprachlichen Unterricht. Mit dem Beiblatt "Phonetische Studien." Published by Wilhelm Viëtor (with collaboration of Franz Dörr and Adolf Rambeau). Marburg. Since 1893. Yearly ten parts. (12s. a year.)

8. *Zeitschrift für Französischen und Englischen Unterricht.* Edited by M. Kaluza, E. Koschwitz (+), G. Thurau. Berlin. Since 1902. Yearly 6 parts. (10s. a year.)

9. *Neuphilologisches Zentralblatt.* Organ der Vereine für Neuere Sprachen in Deutschland. Monthly. xx vols. Since 1887. 1906. Hannover. (8s. a year.) (Now discontinued.)

10. *Zeitschrift für den Deutschen Unterricht*, begründet unter Mitwirkung von Rudolf Hildebrand, herausgegeben von Otto Lyon. Leipzig. Since 1887. Monthly. (12s. a year.)

11. *Wissenschaftliche Beihefte zur Zeitschrift des Allgemeinen Deutschen Sprachvereins.* Berlin. Verlag des Sprachvereins. Cheap and valuable. Up to November, 1905 : 27 Hefte.

12. *Zeitschrift für Französische Sprache und Litteratur*, originally *Zeitschrift für Neufranzösische Sprache und Litteratur*, mit besonderer Berücksichtigung des Unterrichts,im Französischen auf den deutschen Schulen, herausgegeben von G. Körting und E. Koschwitz. The present general editor is D. Behrens. Oppeln und Leipzig. (Now Berlin.) Since 1879. This periodical is no longer devoted exclusively to *Modern* French. (15s. a year.)

13. *Litteraturblatt für Germanische und Romanische Philologie*, herausgegeben von Otto Behagel und Fritz Neumann. Leipzig. Since 1880. Monthly. (11s. a year.)

14. *Monatsschrift für Höhere Schulen.* Edited by R. Köpke and A. Matthias. Berlin. Weidmann. Since 1902. Monthly. (15s. a year.)

15. *Revue de l'Enseignement des Langues Vivantes.* Edited by
A. Wolfromm. Paris. Since 1883. (15s. a year.) Monthly.

16. *Bulletin mensuel* de la Société des professeurs de langues
vivantes de l'enseignement public. Paris. Now edited by
G. Camerlynck and called *Les Langues Modernes.* Monthly.
Since 1903.

17. *Le Maître Phonétique,* organe de l'Association Phonétique
Internationale. Edited by Paul Passy, Bourg-la-reine (near
Paris). Assistant Editor, D. Jones, 7 Copse Hill, Wimbledon.
Six numbers a year. Since 1886. (4s. a year, or 2s. 10d. for
members of the International Phonetic Association.)

REPORTS.

1. *Verhandlungen der Deutschen Neuphilologentage.* Every
alternate year one volume of Proceedings. Vols. I—X.
Hannover. Since 1886. Vol. XIII. Hannover. 1909. 3s.
English teachers of modern foreign languages will find the
study of the Proceedings at the German Neuphilologentage
very suggestive, and directly useful.

2. *Jahresberichte für das höhere Schulwesen.* Edited by K.
Rethwisch. Berlin. Weidmann. Since 1886. One vol.
yearly. (Price varying from 10s. to 15s.)

3. *Special Reports on Modern Language Teaching.* [Education
Department] London. Several volumes, since 1899.

4. *Report of the Committee of Twelve* of the Modern Language
Association of America. With introduction by the Chairman,
Calvin Thomas. Boston. 1900.

5. *Report of the Committee of Nine* of the Modern Language
Association of America, to consider the advisability and
feasibility of extending the High School course in German.
Prepared by Prof. A. R. Hohlfeld. Madison. 1905.

6. *Full reports of the proceedings of the (English) Modern
Language Association* and of papers read at their general
meetings used to be given in "The Modern Language
Quarterly," and are now found in "The Modern Language
Review" and in "Modern Language Teaching." See also the
helpful notices in the "Journal of Education."

7. *Suggestions for a Modern Language Curriculum.* Report by a Special Sub-committee of the Education Sub-committee of the Incorporated Association of Assistant Masters, with the assistance of three co-opted members on an Ideal Curriculum in Modern Languages. (November, 1905.) See "Modern Language Teaching," I (1905), 241—5.

8. *Report on the Conditions of Modern (Foreign) Language Instruction in Secondary Schools.* See "Modern Language Teaching," Vol. IV (1908), Nos. 2 and 3.

9. *Report on the Qualifications and Training of Modern Language Teachers.* See "Modern Language Teaching," Vol. V (April, 1909), 65—77. See also "Journal of Education," April, 1909.

10. Resolutions regarding the position of Modern Languages in Scottish Schools and Universities, adopted by the Scottish Modern Languages Association, and preceded by a 'Memorandum' explanatory of the 'Resolutions.' Edinburgh. October, 1908. See also "Modern Language Teaching," IV (1908), 198—201.

BOOKS, PAMPHLETS AND ESSAYS[1].

1. *Allcock (A. E.).* The Teaching of Modern Languages (in "Essays on Secondary Education by various contributors," ed. Chr. Cookson, pp. 149 sqq.). Oxford. 1898. (4s. 6d. cloth.)

2. *Atkinson (H. W.).* An Experiment in Modern Language Teaching (*Journal of Education*, May, 1897). On the articles by F. B. Kirkman; his reply is contained in the *Journ. of Educ.* June, 1897. See nos. 21 and 22.

---

[1] The books, pamphlets and essays enumerated are equal in value and not invariably written from the same point of view, nor do they always agree with the views set forth in the preceding pages, but they will all be found suggestive and helpful. These lists do not comprise all that is worth reading on the subject, their aim being simply to point out a large number of recent contributions to the study of Methods of Modern Language Teaching, to which teachers will find it useful to refer. For further information see Münch's and Glauning's book (described under 43) which gives very valuable bibliographical lists. The books most useful for the teacher of German are discussed on pp. 115 sqq. Cp. also the Bibliography in Bagster-Collins, pp. 224 sqq. (described under 3 in this list).

3. *Bagster-Collins* (*Elijah W.*). The Teaching of German in Secondary Schools. New York and London. Macmillan. 1904. (6*s*. 6*d*. net.)

4. *Bahlsen* (*Leopold*). The Teaching of Modern Languages. (Translation by M. B. Evans.) Boston. Ginn. No year [1905]. (2*s*. 6*d*.)

5. *Baumann* (*Fr.*). Reform und Antireform im Neusprachlichen Unterricht. Berlin. 1902. (1*s*. unbound.)

6. *Bell* (*G. C.*). The Relative Advantages of Different Systems of Modern Language Teaching (a paper read at the Headmasters' Conference, Cambridge, Dec. 1901 and published as a pamphlet).

7. *Braunholtz* (*E. G. W.*). Books of Reference for Students and Teachers of French. London. Hachette. 1902. (2*s*. 6*d*.)

8. *Bréal* (*Michel*). De l'enseignement des langues vivantes. Paris. 1900. (frcs 2 unbound.)

9. *Brebner* (*Mary*). The Method of Teaching Modern Languages in Germany. London. 1898. (1*s*. 6*d*. cloth.) See also : Sadler's Reports, Vol. III (1898), no. 8.   (3*s*. 6*d*. net.)

10. *Brereton* (*Cloudesley*). The Teaching of Modern Languages with special reference to big towns. London. Blackie. 1905. (1*s*.)

11. *Breul* (*Karl*). The Training of Teachers of Modern Foreign Languages. Lecture delivered at the College of Preceptors. (*Educational Times*, May, 1894.) See now pages 86 sqq.

12. *Breul* (*Karl*). Speeches on the needs of Modern Languages delivered at Cambridge (see *Mod. Lang. Quarterly*) and in London (see *M. L. Q.* IV. 2 (July, 1901) pp. 156—8). See also *The Times*, Dec. 26th, 1900—Jan. 29th, 1901, *Sapere Aude*, "The means of encouraging the Study of Modern Languages"; also *Journal of Education*, April, 1902, "Modern Languages and the Universities,—Supply of Teachers"; also *Morning Post* (Oct. 31st and Nov. 1st, 1902), "On the teaching of Modern Languages" (reprinted in *The Nation's Need*, pp. 199—222 and 286, edited by Spenser Wilkinson, London, 1903); "The use of the phonograph in Modern Language Teaching" in *Die Neueren Sprachen*, XV (1907), May number. See also p. 110 (note) of this book.

13. *Breul (Karl)*. Greek and its humanistic alternatives in the Little-go. Cambridge. 1905. (1s.)

14. *Breul (Karl)*. A Handy Bibliographical Guide to the Study of German Language and Literature, for the use of students and teachers of German. Hachette. 1895. (2s. 6d. net.)

15. *Breymann (H.)*. Die neusprachliche Reform-Literatur von 1876—93, Leipzig, 1895 (3s. unbound); von 1894—99, Leipzig, 1900 (2s. 3d. unbound); von 1899—1904, Leipzig, 1905 (4s. unbound) The third part is called "Eine bibliographisch-kritische Übersicht," contributed by Prof. Dr Steinmüller.

16. *Carré (Irénée)*. Méthode pratique de langue, de lecture etc. Paris. Colin. 1889. (8d.)

17. *Colbeck (C.)*. On the Teaching of Modern Languages in Theory and Practice. Two Lectures. Cambridge. 1887. (2s. cloth.)

18. *Eggert (Bruno)*. Phonetische und Methodische Studien in Paris. Zur Praxis des neusprachlichen Unterrichts. Leipzig. 1900. (2s. 6d.)

19. *Eggert (Bruno)*. Der psychologische Zusammenhang in der Didaktik des neusprachlichen Reformunterrichts. Berlin. 1904. (1s. 10d.)

20. *Eve (H. W.)*. The Teaching of Modern Languages. (In *National Education*, London, 1901, 228—253.) Reprinted London, 1905. See also *Educ. Times*, February, 1901.

21. *Findlay (J.)*. An Experiment in Modern Language Teaching. (*Journal of Education*, Oct. Nov. Dec. (with A. E. Twentyman), 1896.) See Kirkman, no. 32.

22. *Förster (Max)*. Der Bildungswert der Neueren Sprachen im Mittelschulunterricht. (Lecture delivered at Würzburg on April 13, 1908, reprinted, in an enlarged form, in "Die Neueren Sprachen," Vol. XVI (June, 1908), pp. 129 sqq.

23. *Franke (F.)*. Die praktische Spracherlernung auf Grund der Psychologie und der Physiologie der Sprache dargestellt. Leipzig. 1890. (8d. unbound.)

24. *Frazer (Mrs J. G.)*. The Phonograph as a School appliance. (*Journal of Educ.* Nov. 1905.) See pp. 67—8, and nos. 53 and 57.

25. *Gouin* (*F.*). The art of teaching and studying languages. Translated into English by Swan and Bétis. London. 1892. (7s. 9d.) See no. 37.

26. *Hartmann* (*K. A. M.*). Die Anschauung im neusprachlichen Unterricht. Wien. 1895. (6d. unbound.)

27. *Hartmann* (*K. A. M.*). Reiseeindrücke und Beobachtungen eines deutschen Neuphilologen in der Schweiz und in Frankreich. Leipzig. 1897. (3s. unbound, 4s. cloth.)

28. *Hausknecht* (*Emil*). The Teaching of Foreign Languages. In the Board of Education's " Special Reports on Educational Subjects." Vol. III. no. 9.

29. *Holzer* (*G.*) und *Schmidt* (*G.*). Zur französischen und englischen Unterrichtssprache. Beiträge zu einer Schulphraseologie. Heidelberg. Programm 666. Beilage. Heidelberg. 1900.

30. *Jeffrey* (*P. Shaw*). The study of Colloquial and Literary French. London. Whittaker. 1899. (5s.)

31. *Jespersen* (*Otto*). How to teach a foreign Language. Translated from the Danish original by Sophia Ylsen-Olsen Bertelsen. London. 1904. (3s. 6d.)

32. *Kirkman* (*F. B.*). An Experiment in Modern Language Teaching. (*Journal of Education*, February, April, 1897.) See Findlay; Atkinson.

33. *Kirkman* (*F. B.*). Reform in Modern Language Examinations. (*Journal of Education*, April, 1900, pp. 230 sqq.)

34. *Kirkman* (*F. B.*). Modern Foreign Language Instruction. Principles and Methods. University Tutorial Press. London. To be published presently.

35. *Klinghardt* (*H.*). Ein Jahr Erfahrungen mit der Neuen Methode. Marburg. 1888. (1s. 8d. unbound.)

36. *Klinghardt* (*H.*). Drei weitere Jahre Erfahrungen mit der Neuen Methode. Marburg. 1892. (2s. 6d. unbound.)

37. *Kron* (*R.*). Die Methode Gouin oder das Seriensystem in Theorie und Praxis. Marburg. ²1900. (3s. 6d. bound.) See no. 25.

38. *Lange (Paul).* Zur Reform unserer Neusprachlichen Schulausgaben. Leipzig. 1901. (3½*d.*)

39. *Mangold (W.).* Gelöste und ungelöste Fragen der Methodik, auf dem Gebiet der neueren Fremdsprachen. Berlin. 1892. (8*d.* unbound.)

40. *Mangold (W.).* Der Unterricht im Französischen und Englischen, in the *Reform des Höheren Schulwesens in Preussen.* Halle. 1902. Pp. 191—226, and bibliographical references at end. (12*s.* ; 14*s.* cloth.)

41. *Montgomery (Miss J. D.).* The Teaching of Modern Languages in Belgium and Holland. In Sadler's Reports, Vol. II (1898), no. 26.

42. *Münch (W.).* Zur Förderung des französischen Unterrichts. Heilbronn. 1883. 2nd (improved) edition. Leipzig. 1895. (2*s.* 5*d.* unbound.)

43. *Münch (W.)* und *Glauning (Fr.).* Didaktik und Methodik des französischen und englischen Unterrichts. München. 1895 (from Dr A. Baumeister's "Handbuch der Erziehungs- und Unterrichtslehre für höhere Schulen"). This book contains a most valuable bibliography. (4*s.* 6*d.* unbound.) New separate editions. Münch (1902), Glauning (1903).

44. *Münch (W.).* Welche Ausrüstung für das neusprachliche Lehramt ist vom Standpunkte der Schule aus wünschenswert? (In "Die Neueren Sprachen," IV. Heft 6.) Marburg. 1896. (1*s.* 8*d.*) A number of other essays of Münch scattered in various German periodicals are likewise well worth reading.

45. *Münch (W.).* Das Akademische Privatstudium der Neuphilologen, in "Lehrproben und Lehrgänge der Gymnasien und Realschulen." 1905. Separately printed. Halle. 1906. (5*d.*)

46. *Münch (W.).* Die Vorbildung der Lehrer der Neueren Sprachen...Zehn Gebote für junge Neuphilologen. Paper read at the XIIIth Neuphilologentag at Hanover (June, 1908). See p. 60 of this book, note 1.

47. *Neumann (A.).* Führer durch die Städte Nancy, Lille, Caen, Tours, Montpellier, Grenoble, Besançon, für Studierende, Lehrer und Lehrerinnen. Marburg. 1902. (2*s.* bound.)

48. *Ohlert* (*A.*). Die fremdsprachliche Reformbewegung, etc. Königsberg. 1886. (1*s*. 3*d*. unbound.)

49. *Passy* (*Paul*). De la méthode directe dans l'enseignement des langues vivantes. Paris. 1899. (Armand Colin Cie.) (frcs 1.50.)

50. *W. Mansfield Poole*. Method of teaching Modern Languages. (In John Will. Adamson: The Practice of Instruction. London. 1907. 461—504. 4*s*. 6*d*.)

51. *Rippmann* (*Walter*). Hints on Teaching French. London. [4]1906. (1*s*. 6*d*. net, boards.) Hints on Teaching German. London. 1899. [3]1906 (rewritten). (1*s*. net, boards.)

52. *Rippmann* (*Walter*). On the Early Teaching of French. (A series of articles in Macmillan's "School World," beginning in no. 1.)

53. *Rippmann* (*Walter*). The Production of artificial speech sounds. (In the *School World*, April, 1906.) See no. 57.

54. *Roden* (*A. v.*). In wiefern muss der Sprachunterricht umkehren? Ein Versuch zur Verständigung über die Reform des neusprachlichen Unterrichts. Marburg. 1890. (1*s*. 8*d*. unbound.) See nos. 75 and 80.

55. *Roden* (*A. v.*). Die Verwendung von Bildern zu französischen und englischen Sprechübungen, methodische Ansichten und Vorschläge. Marburg. 1898. (1*s*. 3*d*. unbound.)

56. *Rossmann* (*P.*). Ein Studienaufenthalt in Paris. Ein Führer für Studierende, Lehrer und Lehrerinnen. Third ed. called "Handbuch für einen Studienaufenthalt im französischen Sprachgebiet." Marburg. 1907. (3*s*. 3*d*. bound.)

57. *Rouse* (*W. H. D.*). The Phonograph in the Class-Room. (Illustrated.) The *School World*, May, 1906. (6*d*.)

58. *Rouse* (*W. H. D.*). Translation. *The Classical Review*, June, 1908. (1*s*.) And also "Classical Work and Method in the Twentieth Century," in "Rivista di Scienza 'Scientia.'" Vol. IV. Anno II (1908). No. VII. Bologna. N. Zanichelli. 1908.

59. *Sallwürck* (*E. v.*). Fünf Kapitel vom Erlernen fremder Sprachen. Berlin. 1898. (1*s*. 5*d*.)

60. *Savory (D. L.).* Progress of the Reform Method of Teaching Modern Languages, in *Speaker,* Sept. 23rd, 1905. (Cp. article by same writer in *Speaker,* Sept. 19th, 1903.)

61. *Schlapp (Otto).* Modern Languages in Scotch Schools and Universities, their present position and prospects. Edinburgh. 1899. See p. 117, under 10.

62. *Schlapp (Otto).* The Report of the Scottish Universities Commission and the place of Modern Languages in the Examinations for Bursaries of the Scottish Universities. Edinburgh. Darien Press. 1900. (3*d.*) See p. 117, under 10.

63. *Schweitzer (Ch.).* Méthodologie des langues vivantes. Paris. A. Colin.

64. *Siepmann (Otto).* The advantages and fallacies of the new method of teaching French. (An address delivered in London, Dec. 1903.) Reprinted from the *Preparatory Schools Review.* Oxford. Bocardo Press. 1904.

65. *Siepmann (Otto).* Modern Languages as an instrument of Education and Culture. (A paper read at Oxford, April, 1904.) London. Hodgson Co. 1904. [Reprinted in the "Zeitschrift für französischen und englischen Unterricht." 1905.]

66. *Siepmann (Otto).* Preface to his "Primary French Course." London. 1902.

67. *Sigwalt (Ch.).* De l'enseignement des langues vivantes. Paris. 1906. (3*s.* unbound.)

68. *Skinner (M. M.).* In wieweit darf man sich beim Unterricht in der deutschen Sprache des Übersetzens ins Englische bedienen? In the American "Monatshefte für deutsche Sprache und Pädagogik." Januar und Februar, 1908.

69. *Soltmann (H. C.).* Der fremdsprachliche französische Unterricht an der Höheren Mädchenschule. Leipzig. 1889. (1*s.* unbound.)

70. *Soltmann (H. C.).* Das propädeutische Halbjahr des französischen Unterrichts in der Höheren Mädchenschule. Bremen. 1893. (1*s.* 6*d.* unbound.)

71. *Spencer (Fr.).* Chapters on the aims and practice of teaching. Chapter III. (French and German, by the general editor.) Cambridge. 1897. (6*s.* cloth.)

72. *Spieser* (*J.*). Ein Klassenversuch mit der begrifflichen Methode im ersten Leseunterricht. Leipzig. K. G. T. Scheffer. 1904.

73. *Storr* (*Fr.*). The Teaching of Modern Languages (French and German) in "Teaching and Organisation, with special reference to Secondary Schools. A manual of practice, edited by P. A. Barnett." London. 1897. Pp. 261—280. At the end of this essay some other contributions by Mr. Storr to the question of Modern Language Teaching are enumerated. See also *A. T. Pollard's* remarks on pp. 24—6 of the same volume. (6s. 6d. cloth.)

74. *Sweet* (*H.*). The Practical Study of Languages. London. 1899. New York. 1900. (6s. net.)

75. *Tanger* (*G.*). Muss der Sprachunterricht umkehren? Berlin. 1888. (9d. unbound.) See nos. 54 and 80.

76. *Thiergen* (*Oscar*). Methodik des neusprachlichen Unterrichts. Leipzig. 1903. (4s. 3d. cloth.)

77. *Thomas* (*Calvin*), A. Marshall Elliott, W. Stuart Macgowan and others. Methods of Teaching Modern Languages. Boston, U. S. A. 1891. (Essays and speeches very unequal in value and importance. 3s. 6d. cloth.)

78. *Tuke* (*Margaret J.*). Article in *Journal of Education*, November, 1902.

79. *Veyssier* (*E.*). De la méthode pour l'enseignement scolaire des langues vivantes. Paris. 1898. (3s.)

80. *Viëtor* (*W.*). (Quousque Tandem.) Der Sprachunterricht muss umkehren. Heilbronn. 1882. Third ed. with additional notes, 1905. (8d. unbound.) See nos. 54 and 75.

81. *Viëtor* (*W.*). Die Methodik des neusprachlichen Unterrichts. Ein geschichtlicher Überblick in vier Vorträgen. Leipzig. 1902. (1s. unbound.) See also p. 86 (note) of this book.

82. *Viëtor* (*W.*). Wissenschaft und Praxis in der neueren Philologie. Marburg. 1899. (5d. unbound.)

83. *Waetzoldt* (*St.*). Die Aufgabe des Neusprachlichen Unterrichts und die Vorbildung der Lehrer. Berlin. 1892. (1s. unbound.) With regard to this very important paper compare the "Verhandlungen des fünften allgemeinen deutschen

Neuphilologentages zu Berlin" (1892) (Hannover, 1893, pp. 25 sqq.) and the reviews of Waetzoldt's lecture in " Die Neueren Sprachen," I. 48 sqq. (Viëtor) ; " Mitteilungen zur Anglia," III. 361 sqq. (Wendt) ; "Zeitschr. für französische Sprache," XIV. I sqq. (Stengel); "Englische Studien," XIX. 137 sqq. (Kölbing) ; "Litteraturblatt für germanische und romanische Philologie," XV. 130 sqq. (Koschwitz).

84. *Walter (Max)*. Der französische Klassenunterricht. Entwurf eines Lehrplans. Unterstufe. 1888, ²1906. (*1s. 6d.* unbound.) A promised '*Anhang*' to the second edition has not yet appeared.

85. *Walter (Max)*. Englisch nach dem Frankfurter Reformplan. Marburg. 1900. (*3s. 6d.* unbound, bound 4*s.*)

86. *Walter (Max)*. Die Reform des Neusprachlichen Unterrichts auf Schule und Universität. Mit Nachwort von W. Viëtor. Marburg. 1901. (*6d.*)

87. *Walter (Max)*. Der Gebrauch der Fremdsprache bei der Lektüre in den Oberklassen. Marburg. 1905. (*9d.*)

88. *Walter (Max)*. Aneignung und Verarbeitung des Wortschatzes im neusprachlichen Unterricht. Marburg. 1907.

89. *Walter (Max)*. Zur Methodik des neusprachlichen Unterrichts. Vorträge während der Marburger Ferienkurse 1906 und 1908. Marburg. 1908.

90. *Ware (Fabian)*. Phonetics and Modern Language Teaching. (*Journal of Education*, August, 1897.) See Kirkman.

91. *Ware (Fabian)*. The Teacher of Modern Languages in Prussian Secondary Schools. His education and professional training. In Sadler's Reports, Vol. III (1890), no. 10.

92. *Ware (Fabian)*. The Teaching of Modern Languages in Frankfurt a/M. and district. In Sadler's Reports, Vol. III (1898), no. 7.

93. *Widgery (W. H.)*. The Teaching of Languages in Schools. London. 1888. (With a very full chronological bibliography up to 1888.) Reprinted. London. 1903. (*1s.*)

94. *Winch* (*William H.*). Notes on German Schools. London. 1904. (Chapter XV. pp. 162—202, on the teaching of foreign languages in Germany.) (6s. bound.)

95. *Wolfromm* (*A.*). La question des méthodes. Revue de l'enseignement des langues vivantes. Paris. 1902. (April number.)

SPECIAL BOOKS ON THE TEACHING OF GERMAN[1].

96. *Hildebrand* (*R.*). Vom deutschen Sprachunterricht in der Schule. Leipzig. [4]1890. (3s. unbound.)

97. *Laas* (*E.*). Der deutsche Unterricht auf höheren Lehranstalten. Berlin. 1872. [2]1886 (edited by I. Imelmann). (8s. unbound.) See p. 161.

98. *Lehmann* (*Rud.*). Der deutsche Unterricht. Eine Methodik für höhere Lehranstalten. Berlin. 2nd edit. 1897. (9s. cloth.)

99. *Wendt* (*Gustav*). Didaktik und Methodik des deutschen Unterrichts und die philosophische Propädeutik (from Baumeister's 'Handbuch,' Vol. III). 2nd edit. München. 1905. With useful bibliographical lists. (3s. 6d. unbound.)

100. *Matthias* (*Adolf*). Handbuch des deutschen Unterrichts an den höheren Schulen. A monumental work which will ultimately consist of 14 parts, produced by the collaboration of a number of first-rate authorities. München. Seven parts have appeared since 1906.

---

[1] Those books which are specially intended for the use of German teachers in German schools contain much more than an English teacher can possibly expect to get through; but as the smaller is contained in the greater, English teachers of German will in many cases find such works of the utmost service—except in the case of the special conditions and special difficulties of the English learner. With regard to these, and to a detailed account of the method of teaching German in English schools, the best work to consult is at present the American book by E. W. Bagster-Collins. See no. 3 of the foregoing list.

PHONETICS[1].

101. *Klinghardt (H.).* Artikulations- und Hörübungen. Cöthen. 1897. (5*s.* 6*d.* unbound.)

102. *Passy (Paul).* Les sons du Français. Paris. [3]1892. (frcs 1.50 unbound.)

103. *Passy (Paul).* Abrégé de prononciation française. Leipzig. 1897. [2]1901. (1*s.*)

104. *Rippmann (W.).* Elements of Phonetics. English, French, and German. Translated and adapted from Prof. Viëtor's "Kleine Phonetik." London. 1899. (2*s.* 6*d.* net, boards.)

105. *Scholle (W.)* and *Smith (G.).* Elementary Phonetics. English, French, German. Their theory and practical application in the class-room. London. 1903. (2*s.* 6*d.* net.)

106. *Viëtor (W.).* German Pronunciation, Practice and Theory. Leipzig. [3]1903. (2*s.* cloth.) (See pp. 141 of this book.)

107. *Johannson (Arwid).* Phonetics of the New High German Language. Manchester and Leipzig. (3*s.* net.) 1906.

108. *Siebs (Theodor).* Deutsche Bühnenaussprache. Berlin, Köln, Leipzig. [2]1901. (3*s.* 3*d.* bound.) A smaller book is his "Grundzüge der Bühnenaussprache." Ibid. [2]1904. (2*s.* bound.)

109. *Zünd-Burguet (A.).* Méthode pratique, physiologique et comparée de prononciation française, together with a "livret

---

[1] For more detailed information see my *Handy Bibliographical Guide,* pp. 8, 24—6, 35, and also the Index p. 174 of this book. For French, see Braunholtz, "Books of Reference for Students and Teachers of French." London, 1901. Here on pages 32 and 45—7 the titles of the important books by Beyer, Koschwitz, and others are given in full. See also Miss Brebner's pamphlet (No. 5), pp. 70—2, and *Le Maître Phonétique* (January, 1897), pp. 39—41 (ouvrages recommandés pour l'étude de la phonétique et de la pédagogie linguistique). (See also Rippmann in *Modern Language Teaching.*) The larger and very useful works on general Phonetics by Sievers, Trautmann, Viëtor, Jespersen and others are here not enumerated; for some recent books on English phonetics see p. 23.

d'illustrations." Paris and Marburg. 1902. Also by the same
author : "Études de Phonétique Expérimentale." Tome I.
Chez l'auteur. Paris, 48 Rue de Rome. ²1904. "Exercices
pratiques et méthodiques de prononciation française. Spé-
cialement arrangés pour les études pratiques aux universités
et les cours de vacances." Marburg. 1906.

110. *Breymann (H.).* Die phonetische Litteratur von 1876—1895.
Eine bibliographisch-kritische Übersicht. Leipzig. 1897.
(3*s.* 6*d.* unbound.)

111. *Panconcelli-Calzia (G.).* Bibliographia phonetica. Since 1906.
This valuable bibliography forms part of the "Medizinisch-
pädagogische Monatsschrift für die gesamte Sprachheilkunde.
Internationales Zentralblatt für experimentelle Phonetik," edited
by A. and H. Gutzmann. Berlin. Dr G. Panconcelli-Calzia's
work is done at the 'Phonetisches Kabinett' of the University
of Marburg.

THE REFERENCE LIBRARY OF A SCHOOL
TEACHER OF GERMAN[1]

THERE are no doubt many difficulties which beset a teacher
of German in this country, such as—want of time allotted to
his subject in the school curriculum, necessity of preparing his
pupils for a host of examinations, want of a clearly defined
and methodically arranged curriculum, lack of encouragement
of the subject in the vast majority of schools, distinct dis-
couragement in the present regulations for various examinations, shyness of many pupils in dealing with the living and
spoken idiom, uncertainty concerning the best method to be
adopted in teaching, and doubt as to what books should be
used with the classes, and more especially in preparing for
his own work.

It can, however, not be urged that there is not now a great
number of really good, scientific, as well as practical books

[1] Revised and enlarged Reprint from my article in the *Modern
Language Quarterly* for November, 1897, where I was the first to draw up
such lists for English-speaking teachers of German. I had undertaken a
similar task in 1893 by publishing an essay 'Zum Unterricht der Eng-
länder in Deutschland in der deutschen Sprache und Litteratur' in the
'Zeitschrift für den deutschen Unterricht,' Vol. VIII (1894), 155—172. My
lists were followed by O. Siepmann's list of books in 'The School World,'
March, 1901, and W. Rippmann's lists in 'Modern Language Teaching,'
I. 6 (October, 1905), pp. 171. The latter have recently been revised and
printed, in an enlarged form, in 'Modern Language Teaching,' Vols. III
(8), 240 sqq., IV (4), 115 sqq. and IV (5), 151 sqq. They are not so full as
my German lists and do not discuss the books at all, but they deal not only
with German but also with French books.

available for a teacher to refer to in all cases of difficulty and doubt, such as may arise at any moment in the various departments of his everyday teaching. On the contrary, there are, at least in some cases, so many books on the same subject that a real difficulty is experienced by teachers as to which should be used by preference. The school reference libraries are as yet very poor as far as German is concerned, and teachers of German should make every effort to improve them. Apart from this, however, most teachers will probably wish, as far as may be, to purchase gradually all the necessary books of reference for themselves. But as only a very few teachers will be able to possess all the books which they may from time to time wish to consult, the establishment of good school libraries for teachers of modern languages is a pressing need which cannot be ignored any longer.

The choice of tools will, of course, largely depend on the kind of work which the teacher will have to do, but a well-equipped and sufficiently endowed reference library will be found by every teacher of the very greatest importance for the success of his teaching and for necessary self-improvement. It is the object of this article to assist young teachers to some extent in making their choice and in recommending books for school and college libraries. As far as possible the latest editions are quoted. New books of value and interest are, as a rule, noticed in *Modern Language Teaching* and *The Modern Language Review*, as they used to be (since 1897) in the columns of the *Modern Language Quarterly*.

Such ordinary grammars, composition-books, school dictionaries, and the like, as are in daily use in schools, and with which every teacher is naturally familiar, have all, or nearly all, been excluded from the following lists. I shall, in the subsequent paragraphs, freely refer readers to my 'Handy Guide[1],' where a much greater number of books of reference is

[1] Karl Breul, 'A Handy Bibliographical Guide to the Study of the German Language and Literature for the use of Students and Teachers of

given, and will here, once for all, draw attention to a work now in course of publication, which when completed will be of the greatest utility to teachers: the 'Handbuch des deutschen Unterrichts an den höheren Schulen.' (To be completed in about 14 parts, published separately and each complete in itself; General Editor, Adolf Matthias, München. See p. 126.) It contains much that English teachers of German will not require, but a great part of it will be to them, no less than to their German colleagues, of the utmost importance. As it is a very expensive work it will be difficult for most teachers to buy it, but it might well find a place on the shelves of the reference library for modern language teachers in the larger secondary schools. A cheap and useful list of books that deserve to be recommended to German teachers of German to German pupils was compiled by Theodor Matthias under the title 'Zum deutschen Unterricht' (in 'Schriften der Pädagogischen Gesellschaft,' No. 2, Dresden, 1904, 1*s.*), parts of which will also be found useful by teachers on this side of the North Sea.

Dictionaries.—A number of dictionaries of different kinds should be found on the shelves of a well-equipped reference library. Apart from the ordinary small school dictionaries, a teacher will be in constant need of at least one large dictionary of the first order. The last edition of Flügel's well-known and time-honoured dictionary is much to be recommended. Its full title is Felix Flügel, 'Allgemeines Englisch-Deutsches und Deutsch-Englisches Wörterbuch.'

German.' London, Hachette & Co., 1895, 8vo. Bound, 2*s.* 6*d.* Some books enumerated in the present chapter are of more recent date than the 'Guide.' A more recent bibliographical account confined to German literature hails from America. It is J. S. Nollen's very useful 'Chronology and practical bibliography of Modern German Literature.' Chicago, 1903. An excellent list of the best books of reference for a teacher of French was compiled as a counterpart to my 'Guide' by E. G. W. Braunholtz under the title 'Books of Reference for students and teachers of French. A critical survey.' London, Hachette & Co., 1901. 2*s.* 6*d.*

Fourth, entirely remodelled, edition. 2 parts in 3 vols. Braunschweig, 1891. (Price, bd., £2. 5s.)[1] The English-German part is by far the better of the two, it gives many carefully chosen instances from English classical authors of all times, with exact references to the works where they occur, and good German renderings; the German-English part, which is really the more important one for English students, is written on a different plan and leaves more to be desired. A smaller dictionary, partly based on the large Flügel (the English-German part only), is the one called Flügel-Schmidt-Tanger, 'A Dictionary of the English and German Languages for Home and School.' Two vols. London, 1896 (15s. bound). It is excellently printed, very full, marvellously cheap, and most useful for all ordinary purposes.

Still better from a scientific point of view is Schröer's new adaptation of Grieb's well-known dictionary. Berlin, Langenscheidt, [11]1908. 2 volumes bound, 17s.

A work which surpasses even the big Flügel in completeness is the 'Encyclopädisches Englisch-Deutsches und Deutsch-Englisches Wörterbuch,' compiled by Ed. Muret and Daniel Sanders with the help of many specialists. It consists of four volumes, each costing £1. 1s. half-bound. (Berlin, 1891—1902.) An abridged school edition of this most valuable work has also been published. The latest edition of 1908 is very full, having been carefully revised and greatly enlarged by the experienced lexicographer H. Baumann. It is obtainable in two vols. 16s.; in one vol., 15s., Berlin, Langenscheidt, 1908.

The smaller books by Thieme-Kellner, Braunschweig, 1905 (10s., in one volume), and Köhler (which have both been completely re-edited), and the still smaller books by Whitney, Krummacher, James, and Weir (of which I have made and almost rewritten a much enlarged edition called 'Cassell's

---

[1] The prices quoted in this article are those for which the books may be obtained from Messrs Heffer and Sons, Petty Cury, Cambridge. The prices are generally liable to the usual discount.

New German Dictionary' (7s. 6d.), are certainly useful in many respects to school-children and students at the beginning of their course, but do not afford all the information a teacher of German may desire to obtain. Among the host of very small books may be mentioned E. Muret's excellent 'Taschenwörterbuch der Englischen und Deutschen Sprache' (Berlin, ²1902, 3s. 6d.) and Jäschke's handy 'English-German Conversation Dictionary,' which is most useful when travelling in Germany. (London, Nutt, first in 1893. 2s. 6d.)

Apart from German-English and English-German dictionaries, a teacher will often desire to consult a *German dictionary with German explanations*, and, if possible, with well-chosen German instances. The very big works of the brothers Grimm and their successors, and of Daniel Sanders (see my 'Guide,' pp. 48—9), are too bulky and expensive for ordinary purposes; the former is still uncompleted. Two recent dictionaries of smaller size will probably be very welcome to many teachers of German. One is by Moriz Heyne, 'Deutsches Wörterbuch.' 3 vols. Leipzig, 1890–5 (£1. 10s. unbound, £1. 19s. half calf). It contains numerous well-chosen instances, and is most handy for reference. A new enlarged edition, giving the latest official spellings, has now been completed, Leipzig, 1905–6. An abridgment of the original edition, in one volume, was published in 1897 (13s. half calf). Another most useful dictionary, in which no full quotations are given, but the development of meaning of the words very carefully elaborated, is the 'Deutsches Wörterbuch,' by Hermann Paul. Halle, 1897, ²1908 (10s. net). Heyne and Paul exclude all foreign words of recent importation. Every teacher should endeavour to get Paul's dictionary and the large Heyne—both will be of daily use to him. Weigand's fine 'Deutsches Wörterbuch' that had been out of print for many years is now being published in a new and thoroughly revised edition. It will be completed in twelve parts and cost about £1. It will then take its place by the side of the works of

Heyne and Paul, each having its peculiar advantages. Up to now 5 parts (A to Käfer, 6s. 6d.) have been published. Teachers anxious to use a German counterpart to Roget's well-known 'Thesaurus of English words and phrases' and Brissière's 'Dictionnaire Analogique' will like to possess Schlessing's 'Deutscher Wortschatz,' Erlangen, 1907 (6s.). English teachers of German will sometimes be in doubt as to the inflexion or pronunciation of *foreign words* in German. They should consult the 'Fremdwörterbuch,' by Daniel Sanders, 2 vols. Leipzig, ²1891–2 (15s. half calf). There is now, however, a strong tendency in Germany to avoid, if possible, the use of foreign words, and several dictionaries have been compiled in which *German equivalents of foreign words* are given. Such are G. A. Saalfeld, 'Fremd- und Verdeutschungswörterbuch,' Berlin, 1898 (7s. 6d. bound), and O. Sarrazin, 'Verdeutschungswörterbuch,' Berlin, ³1905 (6s. bound). Mention should also be made of the 'Verdeutschungswörterbücher des Allgemeinen Deutschen Sprachvereins' (issued to its members). The separate parts are also obtainable at low prices, e.g. Die Speisekarte (i), Der Handel (ii), Die Schule (vii), etc. The most handy dictionary of *synonyms* is Eberhard's 'Synonymisches Handwörterbuch der deutschen Sprache' (the latest, 16th ed., by Otto Lyon) with well-chosen German instances and translations of the German synonyms into English, French, Italian, and Russian. Leipzig, 1904 (half-bound, 13s. 6d.). The *etymology* of words of German origin has been admirably treated by Fr. Kluge in his 'Etymologisches Wörterbuch der deutschen Sprache.' This book, the first edition of which appeared in 1881, has rapidly gone through six carefully revised editions, Strassburg, ⁶1899 (10s. bound). A seventh edition, much enlarged, will be published this year. A short, but useful etymological German dictionary is the one by Ferd. Detter. Leipzig, 1897, ²1909. (Sammlung Göschen, No. 64, 10d. cloth.) A very good *systematical English-German vocabulary* (parts of which will be found useful for private study) has been compiled by Gustav Krüger, 'Englisch-Deutsches Wörterbuch nach Stoffen geordnet für Studierende, Schulen und Selbstunterricht.' Berlin, [2]1895 (3*s.* 10*d.*). A short and systematical 'German Vocabulary for repetition' was compiled by R. H. Dempster (in 'Spiers' Vocabularies for Repetition'). London, 1903 (1*s.* 6*d.*). Very useful 'Picture Vocabularies' for French and German (2 series for each language, at 1*s.* 4*d.* per volume) were published by W. Rippmann. London, Dent. The best known German Dictionary of familiar quotations is G. Büchmann's excellent book 'Geflügelte Worte,' Berlin, [22]1905 (10*s.* bound), and a cheaper book of the same kind is Fried's 'Lexikon deutscher Citate.' Leipzig, Reclam's Universal-Bibliothek, Nos. 2461—3 (1*s.* bound).

Many other dictionaries, including older German dictionaries, special glossaries, dialect dictionaries, dictionaries of technical and commercial words and phrases, etc., which are of less importance for ordinary teaching, must be passed over in this article. Their full titles are given in my 'Guide,' Chapter VI, pp. 45—54. I will only mention F. W. Eitzen's 'Wörterbuch der Handelssprache,' 2 vols. English-German, Leipzig, 1893 (16*s.* bound), which is very full and on the whole reliable, and is not mentioned in the 'Guide.'

Grammars, Books for Beginners, etc.—Such books as are widely known and extensively used in class teaching, e.g. the grammars by Kuno Meyer, Macgowan, Fiedler, Eve, Siepmann, and others, need not be discussed in this place H. G. Fiedler's 'Third German Reader and Writer,' being a First Course of Readings and Exercises on German Syntax (London, Swan Sonnenschein), is, I believe, the only systematic course we have for drill in German Syntax. I wish to call attention to some good books for beginners which seem to be less known. L. Harcourt's 'German for Beginners,' Marburg and London, [3]1906-7 (Part I, 1*s.* 6*d.*, Part II, 2*s.*), is excellent. Very useful are L. D. Savory's 'Deutsches Reformlesebuch,' Oxford, 1908 (2*s.* 6*d.* bound), and K. Wichmann's German story for beginners called 'Am Rhein.' London, 1908 (2s.). The 'Leitfaden für den ersten Unterricht im Deutschen' by S. Alge, with the collaboration of S. Hamburger and W. Rippmann, deserves warm recommendation. A new edition, completely rewritten, has been published in 1905, ²1906, under the title 'Dent's New First German Book,' 2s. 6d. H. G. Atkins' 'Skeleton Grammar of German' (London, Blackie, 1s. 6d.) will be found useful, where it is desirable to emphasize only the main facts of accidence and syntax. The excellent American book by H. C. G. Brandt, 'A Grammar of the German Language for High Schools and Colleges, designed for beginners and advanced students,' Boston, ⁶1893 (6s. net, cloth), which is far too little known in this country, will be found extremely helpful. Teachers should make it a point to obtain the larger edition (including the advanced portion). Among the more bulky works on German grammar written in English, G. O. Curme's 'Grammar of the German Language, designed for a thorough and practical study of the language as spoken and written to-day' (New York, 1905, 15s.), is to be recommended as a useful book of reference. Of those written in German, the 'Neuhochdeutsche Grammatik mit Berücksichtigung der historischen Entwickelung der deutschen Sprache,' by F. Blatz, Karlsruhe, ³1895–6, 2 vols. (entirely rewritten), unbound, 22s., half calf, 25s. 6d., deserves special recommendation. Students and teachers will find Curme and Blatz most useful for study and for reference. They may also like to consult L. Sütterlin's 'Die deutsche Sprache der Gegenwart,' Leipzig, 1900, ²1907, cloth 8s., and the shorter 'Deutsche Sprachlehre für höhere Lehranstalten,' Leipzig, 1905, 2s. 3d. (by L. Sütterlin and A. Waag), both extremely good books. The 'Deutsche Grammatik' (Gotisch, Alt- Mittel- und Neuhochdeutsch), by W. Wilmanns, which is now in course of publication, will probably be of too strictly philological a character to meet the practical needs of schoolteachers. So far Vol. 1 (phonology), Strassburg, ²1897 (8s.

unbound, 10s. half-bound), and Vol. II (word-formation), Strassburg, 1896 (12s. 6d. unbound), and the first half of Vol. III have appeared. A fourth volume, and possibly a fifth, are to follow. It is an admirable piece of work.

An excellent short book for repetition of the principal facts of old and modern phonology and accidence is Fr. Kauffmann, 'Deutsche Grammatik.' Marburg, ³1902 (2s. 9d. cloth). The book is only intended for the use of students, and cannot be used for class teaching. The same holds good of the larger book by Joseph Wright, 'Historical German Grammar,' Vol. I (Phonology, Word-Formation, and Accidence). Oxford, 1907 (5s. bound).

With regard to *syntax* alone, the works by Vernaleken, Erdmann, Kern, and Wunderlich, give much useful information. (See my 'Guide,' p. 32.) Erdmann's work (in two volumes), which is now completed (Vol. II by Otto Mensing, Stuttgart, 1898), deserves special recommendation. (10s. unbound the 2 vols.)

There are a number of German books in which *doubtful points of grammar* and the 'best German' are discussed at length. Five of these will be especially serviceable to English teachers (for others, see my 'Guide,' pp. 29—30). K. G. Andresen, 'Sprachgebrauch und Sprachrichtigkeit im Deutschen.' Ninth edition, Leipzig, 1903 (6s., or cloth 7s.) This is the most conservative book of the five. Th. Matthias, in his 'Sprachleben und Sprachschäden,' Leipzig, ²1897 (6s. 3d. cloth), of which an abridged edition has been published in 1896 (Kleiner Wegweiser durch die Schwankungen und Schwierigkeiten des deutschen Sprachgebrauchs, 1s. 5d.), makes greater concessions to recent usage. The third book is much shorter, but also very useful—A. Heintze, 'Gut Deutsch.' Eighth edition, Berlin, 1897 (1s. 6d. cloth). Heintze has also recently brought out a very large, and on the whole reliable, work in dictionary form on the doubtful points of grammar and style under the title 'Deutscher Sprachhort,' Leipzig, 1900 (12s. unbound), which deserves to be recommended. The last book of this kind is W. Grunow, 'Grammatisches Nachschlagebuch, ein Wegweiser für jedermann durch die Schwierigkeiten der deutschen Grammatik und des deutschen Stils.' Leipzig, 1905 (2s. 6d.).

The fundamental questions concerning the *history of language* in general have been discussed in a masterly way by Henry Sweet in his ' History of Language,' London, Dent, 1900 (1s. net). More detailed books on the subject are Otto Jespersen's 'Progress in Language,' London, 1894 (7s. 6d.), and H. Paul's 'Principien der Sprachgeschichte' (10s. bound). The books (written from different points of view) of Wilh. Wundt, 'Sprachgeschichte und Sprachpsychologie,' Leipzig, 1901 (3s. bound), and B. Delbrück, 'Grundfragen der Sprachforschung' (against Wundt), Strassburg, 1901 (4s. 10d. bound), are of a more advanced character.

Those who wish to have a brief survey of the *history of the German language* and its grammar should refer to O. Weise's ' Unsere Muttersprache, ihr Werden und ihr Wesen' (Leipzig, ⁶1907, 2s. 8d.), to Friedrich Kluge, ' Unser Deutsch, Einführung in die Muttersprache, Vorträge und Aufsätze,' Leipzig, 1907 (bound 1s. 3d.), and also to W. Uhl, 'Entstehung und Entwickelung unserer Muttersprache,' Leipzig, 1906 (1s. 3d.). A somewhat older book of a similar character, and especially good with regard to strictly philological information, is O. Behaghel's ' Die deutsche Sprache' (Leipzig, ⁴1907, revised and enlarged edition) (cloth 4s.). An adaptation of the original edition, which is, however, not free from slips, appeared in London, 1891, under the title, 'A Short Historical Grammar of the German Language' (4s. 6d.). A really first-rate account of the history of the German language considering the special needs of English students of German has still to be written. Teachers may also like to refer to O. Brenner's 'Grundzüge der geschichtlichen Grammatik der deutschen Sprache.' München, 1896 (2s. 5d. unbound). Information on special points is given in A. Waag's 'Bedeutungsentwickelung unseres Wortschatzes' (based on H. Paul's Dictionary), Lahr, 1901 (3*s*. unbound); Albert Polzin's 'Geschlechtswandel der Substantiva im Deutschen (mit Einschluss der Lehn- und Fremdworte),' Hildesheim, 1903. With regard to the vocabulary (especially loan-words) the following books should be consulted:—F. Seiler, 'Die Entwickelung der deutschen Kultur im Spiegel des deutschen Lehnworts' (Halle, I. 1895, [2]1905; II. 1900), 4*s*. the two parts, unbound; R. Kleinpaul, 'Das Fremdwort im Deutschen' (Sammlung Göschen, Leipzig, 10*d*.). A well-written and practical book is the one by Henri Lichtenberger, 'Histoire de la langue allemande.' Paris, 1895 (6*s*.).

Excellent information with regard to niceties of *spelling* is given by W. Wilmanns in his valuable book, 'Die Ortho- graphie in den Schulen Deutschlands.' Berlin, 1887 (3*s*. 8*d*. unbound). It is, however, to some extent superseded by the new 'Reichsorthographie,' and reference should therefore be made to the latest books giving the spellings now officially adopted[1] by Germany, Austria and Switzerland, such as the pamphlet called 'Regeln für die deutsche Rechtschreibung und Wörterverzeichnis,' Berlin, 1902 (3*d*.); K. Duden's handy and reliable 'Orthographisches Wörterbuch der deutschen Sprache mit etymologischen Angaben, kurzen Sacherklärungen und Verdeutschungen der Fremdwörter. Nach den für Deutsch- land, Österreich und die Schweiz gültigen amtlichen Regeln,' Leipzig-Wien, [8]1906 (1*s*. 8*d*.). Otto Sarrazin, in his 'Deutsche Einheitsschreibung,' Berlin, [3]1906 (10*d*.), goes even further, in that he does away with those older spellings which Duden,

---

[1] With regard to English spelling, a moderate and tactful reform, though eminently desirable, cannot be effected by the same simple means as in Germany. Teachers should take an interest in the aims and methods of the recently established (Sept. 1908) 'Simplified Spelling Society,' full information about which can be obtained from its Secretary, Mr W. Archer, 44 Great Russell Street, London, W.C. Its President is the Rev. Professor Skeat, and among the Vice-Presidents and members of Committee are found the names of many of the leading scholars of English in this country. See *M. L. T.* IV. 227 sqq.

following the official regulations, in some cases allowed as alternatives. Sarrazin justly believes that two ways of spelling the same word should be discouraged and only prints the more modern spelling in all cases of doubt. Aug. Vogel, 'Ausführliches Grammatisch-orthographisches Nachschlagebuch,' Berlin, 1902, 2s. 10d. bound, is also a most useful book of reference written on a different plan from Duden's which teachers may sometimes like to consult by the side of Duden's book. They should also read what has been forcibly urged by Otto Siebs in his 'Zur Einführung der neuen Rechtschreibung,' Breslau, 1903. Valuable critical remarks on spelling are to be found in a small book by O. Brenner, 'Die lautlichen und geschichtlichen Grundlagen unserer Rechtschreibung.' Leipzig, 1902 (1s. unbound). The differences between the new and the old spelling are well summarised in Johannes Meyer's pamphlet 'Die Abweichungen der neuen von der alten Rechtschreibung,' 2nd ed., Hannover, 1902 (3d.). A short guide to modern *punctuation* is the book by O. Glöde, 'Die deutsche Interpunktionslehre.' Leipzig, 1893 (4d.). Teachers will remember that some attention to German punctuation is indispensable, as in several important points the principles governing English and German punctuation are at variance. Teachers who have to prepare boys for examinations in which they must show proficiency in reading German *handwriting* should use C. F. A. Kolb, 'Lesebuch in Handschriften,' 9th ed., Stuttgart, 1900 (1s. 2d. boards), or H. Oskar Sommer, 'Specimens of German handwriting,' London, Hachette, 1900 (2s. 6d.).

The subject of the best German *pronunciation* is still a very vexed question, even among the Germans themselves. Teachers should refer to pages 66—7 and 97—8, and consult the 'Deutsche Bühnenaussprache' by Th. Siebs, Berlin, ²1901 (3s. 3d. bound), or the abridged edition of this book ('Grundzüge der Bühnenaussprache,' Berlin, ²1904, 2s. 5d. bound) which contains many practical hints as to how common mistakes of pronunciation may be avoided. The books which will be most helpful for English teachers are Viëtor's 'German Pronunciation: Practice and Theory,' Leipzig, ³1903 (2s.), his 'Die Aussprache des Schriftdeutschen,' Leipzig, ⁶1905, with the transcription of the Association Phonétique Internationale (1s. 10d.), and the reprint of his lecture, 'Wie ist die Aussprache des Deutschen zu lehren?' Marburg, ⁴1906 (1s.). A 'Deutsche Lauttafel,' illustrating this lecture, was published at the same time (1s. 6d.). It can also be had on a large scale and mounted to be hung up on the wall of the class-room. Marburg (2s. 6d.). W. Viëtor has just begun to publish his long-promised 'Deutsches Aussprachewörterbuch,' Leipzig, Reisland, 1908 (to be completed in 8 parts, price about 10s. for the whole work). Heinrich Oberländer's 'Übungen zum Erlernen einer dialektfreien Aussprache,' ⁵1900, München (3s. 8d. bound), will also be found very helpful. Teachers who are anxious to consult handy books on *phonetics* may either refer to Arwid Johannson's 'Phonetics of the New High German Language,' Manchester and Leipzig, 1906 (3s.); or to Laura Soames, 'An Introduction to English, French, and German Phonetics, with reading lessons and exercises,' new edition, revised and edited, after Miss Soames' death, by W. Viëtor, London, 1899 (6s.); to Soames' 'Phonetic Method,' 2 parts (each 2s. 6d.); to W. Scholle and G. Smith, 'Elementary Phonetics, English, French, and German, their theory and practical application in the class-room,' London, 1903 (2s. 6d.); to Paul Passy's 'Petite Phonétique comparée des principales langues européennes,' Leipzig and Berlin, Teubner, 1906 (2s. 3d. bound); or to Wilhelm Viëtor's 'Elemente der Phonetik,' Leipzig, ⁵1904 (2s. 10d. cloth). A very useful translation and adaptation of the last mentioned book is Walter Rippmann's 'Elements of Phonetics.' London, ⁴1907 (2s. 6d. net).

Other books and pamphlets on pronunciation and phonetics are: W. Braune, 'Über die Einigung der deutschen Aussprache.' A much discussed Rektoratsrede, Heidelberg, 1904; reprinted Halle, 1905 (1s. 3d.). Karl Luick, 'Deutsche Lautlehre, mit besonderer Berücksichtigung der Sprachweise Wiens und der Österreichischen Alpenländer' (Leipzig-Wien, 1904, 2s. 6d.). H. Huss, 'Lehre vom Accent der deutschen Sprache, zum erstenmal vollständig behandelt und für Fremde bearbeitet' (Altenburg, 1877, 1s. 3d.). G. Hempl, 'German orthography and phonology' (Boston, U.S.A., 1897, 9s.). C. H. Grandgent, 'German and English Sounds' (Boston, U.S.A., 1892, 2s. 6d.). For the use of those who are anxious to study German texts of an easy character in phonetic transcription W. Viëtor has written a 'Deutsches Lesebuch in Lautschrift,' Part I, ²1904 (3s. bound); Part II, 1902 (3s. bound). Leipzig and London (Nutt). There exists an edition of Schiller's 'Wilhelm Tell' in phonetic script by Pierce-Hempl. New York (Hinds-Noble), 1900. Mention may here be made also of the 36 German phonographic records (in 3 sets), spoken by me for Mrs J. G. Frazer's series (1906) (apply to Mrs Frazer, St Keyne's, Grange Road, Cambridge), which will be found a help to individual teachers preparing for their work as well as to classes of moderate size. The records aim at giving as far as possible a model pronunciation of a considerable number of carefully selected and graduated specimens of German prose and poetry. They should be several times repeated by the phonograph till the scholars are familiarized with every sound and have also caught the accent of the phrase and have understood the proper way of reciting German prose and verse.

There are several books devoted to the teaching of *conversation* (see my 'Guide,' p. 38). Perhaps the most serviceable of them is A. Hamann's 'Echo of Spoken German,' Leipzig, 1892 (2s. 6d. cloth), a series of excellent dialogues, which afford, at the same time, a useful introduction to the study of German life and manners. With regard to the latter, R. Kron's 'German Daily Life' (London, ⁴1905) (2s. 6d. net), and also the 'Bilder deutschen Lebens und Wesens' by the same author (Karlsruhe, 1905, 1s. 3d. bound), will be found interesting.

For the explanation of German *idiomatic phrases*, no better books could be desired than those by Wilh. Borchardt, 'Die sprichwörtlichen Redensarten im deutschen Volksmunde nach Sinn und Ursprung erläutert,' Leipzig, ⁵1895 (by G. Wustmann) (7s. cloth), and by H. Schrader, 'Der Bilderschmuck der deutschen Sprache.' Berlin. Sixth edition, 1901 (7s. cloth). For other similar books, familiar quotations, slang, etc., see my 'Guide,' p. 39, but the smaller books on idioms are, for various reasons, all more or less unsatisfactory. To those enumerated in the 'Guide' might now be added: Martha Bergmann, 'Idioms. Spracheigenheiten, die ein jeder kennen lernen kann und muss. English and German.' 1s. Paderborn, 1907. (Selbstverlag, bei Frau Martha Bergmann. Paderborn, Kilianstrasse, 26.) This is a very useful little book for beginners in either language—every piece is given in English and in German and a few questions on each piece are added. Larger and differently arranged are M. Taker and F. F. Roget, 'German Idioms,' London, 1906 (3s. 6d.); A. Oswald, 'A Selection of German Idioms and Proverbs.' London, 1902 (1s. 6d.). Still a really good book for English students remains to be written.

Teachers who make their advanced pupils write *free essays* on German classical works or characters occurring in great plays should use among others the books of Victor Kiy, 'Themata und Dispositionen zu deutschen Aufsätzen und Vorträgen im Anschluss an die deutsche Schullektüre für die oberen Klassen höherer Lehranstalten,' three parts, Berlin, 2nd ed. 1897–9 (Parts I and III 3s., Part II 3s. 6d. cloth). Other good books are H. Ullrich, 'Deutsche Muster-Aufsätze' (Leipzig, ²1903, 2s. 10d. unbound); Karl Küffner, 'Aufsatzbuch' (Nürnberg, 1905, 3s. unbound); Julius Naumann, 'Theoretisch-praktische Anleitung zur Besprechung und Abfassung deutscher Aufsätze' (Leipzig-Berlin,⁸1907, cloth 4s. 10d.); and L. Teetz, 'Aufgaben aus deutschen epischen und lyrischen Gedichten' (Leipzig, Engelmann), a number of cheap and most excellent little volumes (varying in price between 9d. and 2s.).

For the teaching of *scientific German* nothing can be better than 'A first German course for science students,' comprising a Reader and outline of grammar with diagrams and vocabulary, by H. G. Fiedler and F. E. Sandbach, London, 1906 (2s. 6d.). It has been followed by 'A second German course for science students, Readings from German scientific publications,' by the same authors, London, 1906 (2s. 6d. net). There is also 'A German Science Reader with Notes and Vocabulary' by W. H. Wait. New York, 1907 (4s. 6d.).

For instruction in *Commercial* correspondence teachers may avail themselves, among others, of E. E. Whitfield and C. Kaiser, 'A Course of Commercial German,' London, 1903 (3s. 6d.) or of the recent books by F. E. Sandbach, 'Commercial Correspondence,' Leipzig, 1908 (bound 3s. 6d.), or the 'Handbook of German Commercial Correspondence,' by F. Bithell, London, 1908 (bound 3s. 6d.), which seem to be excellent.

Histories of Literature.—The best history of German literature written in English is the one by John G. Robertson (Edinburgh and London, 1902, 10s. 6d. net). In a second edition of this excellent book the relations between German and English literature and the most significant parallels and differences between the two might with advantage be more strongly emphasised. A suggestive book giving an account of the development of German literature as influenced by social forces has hailed from America. It was originally called 'Social Forces in German Literature. A study in the history of Civilization,' by Kuno Francke, which title has in the English edition been altered to 'A History of German Literature as determined by Social Forces,' London, 1901, ⁶1903 (10s. cloth). The older books in English are of little or no value, and the English adaptations of German works are none of them free from very serious shortcomings. Hence a teacher will very likely prefer to possess one or more German works of moderate size on the subject. The following will, in my opinion, best serve his purpose—Wilhelm Scherer, 'Geschichte der deutschen Litteratur,' Berlin, 11th ed., 1908 (10s. cloth), perhaps the most brilliant book of its kind, written by a ripe scholar, who was endowed with a refined taste for literary beauty. A good book the final portion of which has not yet appeared is the one by Alfred Biese, 'Deutsche Literaturgeschichte.' 2 vols. Munich, 1907–8 (11s.). The concluding volume will probably be published before long. Another very valuable work is the 'Geschichte der deutschen Litteratur von den ältesten Zeiten bis zur Gegenwart,' by Friedrich Vogt and Max Koch. Leipzig and Wien, 1897, ²1904, 2 vols. (£1). This book is profusely adorned with very carefully selected and splendidly executed illustrations, giving facsimiles of old and modern manuscripts and handwritings, and numerous portraits of famous authors, etc. The scientific value of this book is incomparably higher than that of another well-illustrated history of literature by Robert König (26th revised ed. in two vols. Bielefeld and Leipzig, 1898) (£1 half calf), which has still a wide circulation in Germany. A splendid large picture-book, merely illustrating German literature from the earliest times to the present day by over 2200 pictures and illustrations, is Gustav Könnecke's 'Bilderatlas zur Geschichte der deutschen Nationalliteratur. Ergänzung zu jeder deutschen Litteraturgeschichte.' 2nd ed. Marburg, 1895 (£1. 8s.). It is marvellously cheap for what it contains. A popular edition of the big work has just been published, called Könnecke-Muff, 'Deutscher Litteraturatlas. Eine Volksausgabe des grossen Bilderatlas...' With 800 illustrations, many of which are full page and coloured. 1908 (6s. bound). There is a recent book by S. R. Nagel, 'Deutscher Litteraturatlas. Die geographische und politische Verteilung der deutschen Dichtung in ihrer Entwickelung, nebst einem Anhang von Lebenskarten der bedeutendsten Dichter. Auf 15 Haupt- und 30 Nebenkarten.' Wien and Leipzig, 1907 (boards 6s.). For German Literature as seen by a French critic, see A. Bossert, 'Histoire de la littérature allemande' (2nd, revised ed., Paris, 1904, 4s. bound), which is a very interesting and helpful book. A model of the way in which special studies in literature should be written is Charles Herford's 'Literary Relations of England and Germany in the XVIth century' (Cambridge University Press, 1886, 9s.). Advanced students of the older periods of literature will find Marion Edward's 'Summary of the Literature of Modern Europe to 1400,' London, 1907 (7s. 6d.), very useful.

For the eighteenth century the great work by H. Hettner, 'Geschichte der deutschen Litteratur im achtzehnten Jahrhundert,' 4th ed. (revised by O. Harnack), Braunschweig, 1894 (£1. 15s. 6d. unbound, or bound in 2 vols. (leather) £1. 19s. 6d.), will be found as useful as it is interesting. For the two last centuries all necessary personal and bibliographical references are given in the second edition of Karl Goedeke's admirable 'Grundrisz' which after Goedeke's death is being continued by a number of leading German scholars. 8 vols. unbound. Vol. 9 is in course of publication. A shorter but most useful book is Adolf Bartels, 'Handbuch zur Geschichte der deutschen Literatur.' Leipzig, [2]1908 (5s.). There are not a few books from which information as to German literature in the nineteenth century can be obtained. It is hardly necessary to say that they differ a great deal in character and judgment, but in most of them there is plenty of interesting matter and valuable information. I must pass over a number of such works but should like to draw the attention of teachers of German to the following : Richard M. Meyer, Die deutsche Litteratur des neunzehnten Jahrhunderts. Berlin, 1900, [3]1906 (rewritten, 12s. 6d. bound). This is a very valuable book written by one of the most gifted pupils of Scherer. It is the outcome of a stupendous amount of reading and suggestive on every page even if one cannot always agree with the views of the learned author. Most useful bibliographical references are contained in the same author's 'Grundriß der neueren deutschen Litteraturgeschichte.' Berlin, 1902, [2]1908 (7s. bound). Older books are R. v. Gottschall, 'Die deutsche Nationallitteratur des neunzehnten Jahrhunderts. Litterarhistorisch und kritisch dargestellt.' 6th ed., 4 parts. Breslau, 1892 (£1 unbound). Ad. Stern, 'Studien zur Litteratur der Gegenwart' (with portraits of authors). Dresden and Leipzig, ³1905 (10s. 6d. unbound, 12s. 6d. cloth). A second volume (Neue Folge) appeared at Dresden and Leipzig in 1904 (12s. 6d. cloth). The book by John Firman Coar, 'Studies in German literature in the nineteenth century,' New York, 1903 (10s. 6d. net, bound), is interesting and contains many excellent observations. It should, however, be noted, that it is written 'with the intention to measure the development of the German nation by ideals of American democracy, though not by standards of American living.' A short but useful account of recent German literature is given by Carl Weitbrecht under the title 'Deutsche Litteraturgeschichte des 19. Jahrhunderts' (Sammlung Göschen), 2 vols., 1901 (bound 1s. 8d.). The short account of nineteenth-century literature by Adolf Stern, 'Die deutsche Nationallitteratur vom Tode Goethes bis zur Gegenwart' (originally intended to form a supplement to Vilmar's 'History of German Literature'), Marburg, ⁶1908, is also to be recommended (3s. cloth). Another interesting book is the one by Adolf Bartels, 'Die deutsche Dichtung der Gegenwart. Die Alten und die Jungen.' Leipzig,⁷1907 (5s. cloth). A short introduction to 19th century German literature for beginners is Weicher's 'Deutsche Literaturgeschichte,' Part II (the nineteenth century). Leipzig, 1907 (1s. 3d. cloth). Books dealing with the various departments of literature in detail— the novel, the drama, lyric poetry, etc.—cannot be enumerated here. The titles of many of the more important ones will be found in chapters 8 and 12 of my 'Handy Guide.' From a great number of German primers of literature for beginners only those by H. Kluge, Max Koch, G. Bötticher and K. Kinzel, Weicher, and Gotthold Klee (Dresden and Berlin, ²1907, 2s.) need be mentioned. See my 'Guide,' pp. 63—4. Each has its own advantages. Klee's and Weicher's books seem to be the best for school purposes.

Metre.—A short but useful survey of the history of German metre, with good specimens and due consideration of modern forms, is given by Fr. Kauffmann in his ' Deutsche Metrik nach ihrer geschichtlichen Entwickelung.' Marburg, 1897 (4s. 3d.). A more detailed account of modern German metre—a subject which apparently is hardly ever touched upon in school teaching, while the outlines of it deserve to be just as well known as the metrical art of the ancient classical writers—is given in F Minor's ' Neuhochdeutsche Metrik.' Strassburg, [2]1902 (10s. unbound; 12s. half calf). Most teachers will probably find the book too elaborate for their purpose in spite of its being extremely readable and suggestive. The metre of a play in blank verse and in the Old German free metre of four accents is fully discussed in my edition of Schiller's 'Wallenstein I.' Cambridge, [2]1896 (3s. 6d. cloth); blank verse alone in my editions of 'Wilhelm Tell,' Cambridge, [2]1897 (2s. 6d. cloth), and of Goethe's 'Iphigenie,' Cambridge, 1899 (3s. 6d. cloth).

Theory of Poetry, etc.—A number of ' Poetiken' of very different size and character are enumerated in my 'Guide' on pp. 74—5. There will be little time, and indeed little need, for systematic instruction in the theory of poetry in our schools, but teachers will probably like to possess and use at least the following small and cheap hand-book: C. F. A. Schuster, ' Lehrbuch der Poetik für höhere Lehranstalten,' Halle, 3rd ed. 1890 (2s. cloth). In this connection I should like to mention and to recommend very strongly three books which teachers will find helpful in preparing discussions of the classical German dramas with more advanced pupils. They are: Gustav Freytag, ' Die Technik des Dramas,' 9th ed. Leipzig, 1901 (5s. unbound, 6s. 6d. bound) ; the American translation of this book by E. J. MacEwan, Chicago, 1895 (7s. 6d. cloth), does not seem to be very well done. R. Franz, ' Der Aufbau der Handlung in den klassischen Dramen,' Bielefeld and Leipzig, [2]1898 (4s. 6d. unbound, 6s. half-bound). H. Bulthaupt, ' Dramaturgie des Schauspiels,' Vol. 1

(Lessing, Goethe, Schiller, Kleist). Oldenburg and Leipzig, 9th ed. 1902 (7*s.* cloth). Paul Goldscheider's 'Erklärung deutscher Schriftwerke in den oberen Klassen höherer Lehranstalten' (Berlin, 1889, 1*s.* 6*d.* unbound, and a 'Nachtrag' published in 1893), and his recent book 'Lesestücke und Schriftwerke im deutschen Unterricht' (München, 1906, 8*s.*, cloth 9*s.*), will also be found useful.

Among the numerous *prose readers* the following will be found suitable for advanced students and of interest to the teachers themselves : Wilhelm Paszkowski, 'Lesebuch zur Einführung in die Kenntnis Deutschlands und seines geistigen Lebens, für ausländische Studierende und für die oberste Stufe höherer Lehranstalten des In- und Auslands' (Berlin, ⁴1909, 3*s.* 3*d.* cloth, with excellent notes). Margarete Henschke, 'Deutsche Prosa, ausgewählte Reden und Essays, zur Lektüre auf der obersten Stufe höherer Lehranstalten zusammengestellt' (Leipzig-Berlin, 1905, 3*s.* 6*d.* cloth). O. Weise, 'Musterstücke deutscher Prosa, zur Stilbildung und zur Belehrung' (Leipzig Berlin, 1903, 1*s.* 3*d.* cloth). H. Raydt und R. Rössger, 'Deutsches Lesebuch für Handelsschulen und verwandte Anstalten' (Leipzig, 1902, 2*s.* 10*d.* cloth). The latter will be found useful for advanced students of commercial German.

German Classics.—A great number of school editions of German classics with English, German, and French notes are enumerated in my 'Guide,' pp. 94—6. Of English editions without notes Max Müller's anthology 'German Classics' (2 vols.), Oxford, 1886, deserves to be mentioned. Vol. II has been recently revised by F. L. Armitage. (Vol. I, 8*s.* 6*d.* net, Vol. II, 5*s.* 6*d.* net.) Of German editions the Cotta Jubilee edition of Schiller's and Goethe's works is excellent (Schiller in 16 vols. ; Goethe, in 40 vols., cloth, 2*s.* each). The Hempel editions of Lessing, Goethe and Schiller, now re-edited and published in better print and paper under the title 'Goldene Klassiker Bibliothek,' Deutsches Verlagshaus, Bong and Co., the 'German classics' editions in the Leipzig Bibliographical

Institute (each vol. separately obtainable, well bound, for 2*s*.), Max Hesse's excellent Leipzig editions, and most of the volumes of Kürschner's 'Deutsche National-Litteratur' and of Brockhaus' 'Bibliothek der deutschen Nationallitteratur des achtzehnten und neunzehnten Jahrhunderts,' deserve to be recommended. Of the cheap series the volumes of Cotta's 'Bibliothek der Weltlitteratur' (bound 1*s*.), those of the 'Collection Spemann' (bound 1*s*.), are printed in excellent type on good paper. Heyse and Laistner's Deutscher und Neuer Deutscher Novellenschatz, and the capital volumes of the Deutsche Dichter-Gedächtnis-Stiftung, Hamburg-Grossborstel, can be had for 1*s*. each; the well-known series of novels, original and translated from many foreign languages, which is called 'Engelhorn's Allgemeine Roman-Bibliothek' (Stuttgart), each vol. 6*d*. unbound, and 10*d*. bound; the still cheaper 'Deutsche Bücherei' (Berlin), each vol. 3*d*. unbound, and 6*d*. bound; the Hendel editions (Halle), for 3*d*. per volume; Reclam's texts, 'Universal Bibliothek' (Leipzig), 3*d*. per volume; and 'Meyer's Volksbücher' (Leipzig) and the 'Wiesbadener Volksbücher' for 2*d*. per volume, deserve recommendation.

A number of anthologies of modern German *lyric poetry* have been enumerated on pages 98—9 of my 'Guide.' To these I should like to add the following, all of which will be found of moderate compass and worth reading: Carl Busse, 'Neuere deutsche Lyrik,' Halle, 1895 (2*s*. bound); J. Löwenberg, 'Vom goldnen Überfluss,' Leipzig, ⁸1906 (1*s*. 10*d*. bound), with its excellent supplement 'Was die Zeiten reiften (Gedichte aus sechs Jahrhunderten),' Leipzig, 1908 (1*s*. 10*d*.); Adolf Bartels, 'Aus tiefster Seele,' Lahr, ²1897 (4*s*.); Will Vesper, 'Die Ernte aus acht Jahrhunderten deutscher Lyrik,' Düsseldorf and Leipzig, 1906 (1*s*. 10*d*. boards); and the capital selections by Ferdinand Avenarius, 'Hausbuch deutscher Lyrik,' Munich, 1904 (bound 3*s*.), and 'Balladenbuch,' Munich, ²1908 (bound 3*s*. 6*d*.). For children the following deserve to be recommended: G. Falke and J. Löwenberg, 'Steht auf, ihr lieben Kinderlein. Gedichte aus älterer und neuerer Zeit für Schule und Haus ausgewählt,' Köln, Schaffstein. No year (2s.). M. Kühn, 'Macht auf das Tor! Alte deutsche Kinderlieder.' Düsseldorf. 1908 (1s. 10d. bound). R. Kügele, '103 Kinderlieder mit leichter Klavierbegleitung.' Köln, Tonger. No year (1s.). A charming book for beginners is W. Rippmann's 'First Book of German Poetry.' London. 1909 (1s. 6d. bound). A handy edition for school purposes is 'Deutsche Lyrik des neunzehnten Jahrhunderts,' by M. Consbruch and F. Klincksieck, Leipzig, 1903 (2s. bound). A good popular and cheap selection (3d.) is L. Jacobowski's little book, called 'Neue Lieder der besten neueren Dichter fürs Volk,' Berlin, 1899. A delightful anthology of the best German songs, with music, is the one published, under the general editorship of A. R. Hohlfeld, by Messrs Heath and Co. It is called 'Deutsches Liederbuch für amerikanische Studenten,' Boston, 1906. Of German publications I can recommend the following: 'Volksliederbuch für Männerchor, herausgegeben auf Veranlassung Seiner Majestät des deutschen Kaisers Wilhelm II.' 2 vols. Leipzig, Peters, 1907 (6s.). It was the result of the collaboration of a large number of competent workers, above all Johannes Bolte and Max Friedländer. The general editor was Rochus von Liliencron. An excellent 'Kommersbuch' of moderate size is the one edited with critical and historical notes by Max Friedländer. Leipzig, Peters, 2 1897 (1s. 3d.). It contains 180 well-known songs.

For some sets of classics of a more scientific character and some commentaries see my 'Guide,' pp. 81—2 and pp. 100—104.

Old German.—Few teachers will feel inclined to give much time and attention to Old German, and will therefore hardly be in need of advice as to what books to use for the study of the Older German classics. Moreover they will probably have become acquainted with the best books of reference at the Universities where in the future most of our modern language teachers will receive their preliminary training. Still many teachers may at the present moment wish to prepare boys for scholarships at the Universities, and although Old German is with very good reason no longer an indispensable condition for success in an Entrance Scholarship, a teacher may occasionally like to give specially promising pupils a start and teach them the elements of Middle High German or at least some sixteenth century German[1]. Some teachers may also like to continue their own reading and extend their knowledge of Older German literature.

I shall not, in the following list of books, include any works of an advanced character, being strongly of opinion that Old German as such is not a school subject, and should not, unless in very exceptional cases, be begun before the University course. Moreover, a smattering of Old German and German philology, if not carefully taught by an experienced teacher, is sure to do far more harm than good.

The basis of the modern literary language is sixteenth century German. A teacher might first use Raphael Meyer's 'Einführung in das ältere Neuhochdeutsche,' Leipzig, 1894 (1s. 8d.), in which the first fifty-five stanzas of the poem of 'Huernen Seyfrid' are commented on, and then proceed to read some of the small volumes in the handy 'Sammlung Göschen' (Leipzig, 10d. per volume) (see 'Guide,' pp. 79—80). In a similar series, viz. Bötticher and Kinzel's 'Denkmäler der älteren deutschen Literatur,' the volumes 'Hans Sachs' (by K. Kinzel), Halle, ⁴1902 (1s. unbound), and 'Kunst- und Volkslied in der Reformationszeit' (by K. Kinzel), Halle, 1892 (1s. unbound), will be found useful and interesting.

If teachers should desire to give their pupils some specimens of the actual text of Luther's first translation of the Bible ('Septemberbibel') and briefly to discuss the principal changes from sixteenth to nineteenth century German, they cannot do better than choose them from the excellent book by A. Reifferscheid, 'Marcus Evangelion Martin Luthers nach

---

[1] On the whole question see page 102, and my article on 'Modern Languages at Cambridge' in P. Shaw Jeffrey's *The Study of Colloquial and Literary French*, London, 1899, p. 190.

der Septemberbibel, mit den Lesarten aller Originalausgaben, etc.' Heilbronn, 1889 (4*s.* 3*d.* unbound). For other sixteenth century texts nothing can be better than Braune's cheap and reliable 'Neudrucke.' (See 'Guide,' p. 81.)

The best introduction to the study of Middle High German is Julius Zupitza's 'Einführung in das Studium des Mittelhochdeutschen.' Oppeln, 1868. 6th ed., 1901 (2*s.* 6*d.* unbound, 3*s.* cloth). Many scholars have been first initiated into a serious study of Middle High German by a careful perusal of this most excellent little book. After going through Zupitza's practical introduction, teachers might read through Jos. Wright's 'Middle High German Primer,' Oxford, 1888, ²1899 (3*s.* 6*d.*), and then study Hartman von Ouwe's 'Der arme Heinrich' in J. G. Robertson's edition, London, 1895 (2*s.* 6*d.*), or Dr Bieger's annotated edition of the best part of 'Das Nibelungenlied,' Leipzig, ²1908 (3*s.* 6*d.*), or some volumes from Göschen's series. The small Middle High German grammar by H. Paul (Halle, ⁷1908, 3*s.* 9*d.*), and the small M.H.G. dictionary by M. Lexer (Leipzig, ⁶1901, 6*s.*), are much to be recommended.

Mythology, Sagas.—A teacher who is desirous of obtaining a rapid survey of German Mythology and 'Heldensage' without being able to devote much time to the study of the more comprehensive books might read two handy volumes (10*d.* each) of the very useful 'Sammlung Göschen.' The one on 'Deutsche Mythologie' is by Fr. Kauffmann, 2nd ed. Leipzig, 1900; the booklet on 'Die deutsche Heldensage' is by O. L. Jiriczek. Leipzig, ³1906. English translations of these have been made by Miss M. Bentinck-Smith ('Northern Hero Legends,' 1902) and Miss M. Steele Smith ('Northern Mythology,' 1903) in Dent's 'Temple Classics' (1*s.* each). The larger books on these subjects are enumerated in my 'Guide' on pp. 110—112. To these should now be added W. Golther, 'Handbuch der germanischen Mythologie,' Leipzig, 1895 (14*s.* half calf), and O. L. Jiriczek, 'Deutsche Heldensagen,' I, Strassburg, 1898 (8*s.* unbound). The Nibelungen and Kudrun

Sagas have been carefully dealt with by Francis E. Sandbach in 'The Nibelungenlied and Gudrun in England and America,' London, 1904 (10*s.* 6*d.* net), and the Dietrichsage by the same author in his booklet on 'The Heroic saga-cycle of Dietrich of Bern' (Vol. XV of Nutt's 'Popular Studies in Mythology, Romance, and Folklore'), London, 1906 (6*d.*).

Books for Young German readers.—Heinrich Wolgast's book, 'Das Elend unserer Jugendliteratur,' which raised the whole Jugendschriftenfrage, was first published in November, 1896. The third edition of this book (5th and 6th thousand) appeared in March, 1905 (Teubner, Leipzig and Berlin), and costs 3*s.* Since the publication of Wolgast's work giant strides have been made in the direction of providing something better in the way of literary fare for the young than the gaudy but worthless books, whose chief attraction lay in their brilliant covers. No fewer than 67 teachers' associations are co-operating in the selection of good books suitable for the young; and the 'Jugendschriftenwarte,' the organ of the movement (Wunderlich, Leipzig, 12 numbers per annum, 1*s.* 3*d.* yearly), had reached in 1905 a circulation of 50,000 copies. Most of the literature on the subject lies scattered in periodicals; but Wolgast has published a collection of essays, 'Vom Kinderbuche' (Teubner, Leipzig u. Berlin, 1906, 2*s.* 3*d.*); and another collection of essays, 'Zur Jugendschriftenfrage,' herausgegeben von den vereinigten deutschen Prüfungsausschüssen für Jugendschriften (Wunderlich, Leipzig, zweite vermehrte Aufl., 1906, 2*s.*), has a valuable list of books with short critical remarks appended. Each Christmas this 'Verzeichnis empfehlenswerter Jugendschriften,' without the critical apparatus, and with the books grouped according to the age of the children, is given to parents in the different towns in Germany, in the hope that they may be induced to give their children as a present something of lasting literary or artistic value. The scholars' libraries in schools are also being criticized and supplemented upon the same principles as guide the teachers' associations in their selection of books. The whole movement is one of great interest to teachers of German in this country, who will find in those lists many a good and cheap book for their own and for their pupils' reading.

Picture Books, Decorative Wall Pictures.—In March, 1901, an Exhibition, 'Die Kunst im Leben des Kindes,' was held in the Berliner Secessionsgebäude. It consisted of three parts: pictures for decorative purposes, picture-books, and drawings and models made by children. The first two divisions are most important for the teacher of German who desires to have in his class-room pictures illustrating characteristic German scenery and phases of German life, pictures to serve as material for conversation, and picture-books to show to his pupils.

The catalogue of the Exhibition was published in 1901 by Seemann, Leipzig (at 9*d.* unbound), and contains a full bibliography up to that date. No second edition has yet been published. The most important publishers' catalogues of original coloured pictures, 'farbige Künstlersteinzeichnungen,' are those of Teubner, Leipzig u. Berlin, and Voigtländer, Leipzig, containing pictures at prices ranging from 1*s.* to 6*s.*; while the Künstlerbund in Karlsruhe publishes original lithographs and engravings varying in price from 7*s.* 6*d.* to £2 each.

In the domain of the picture-book great progress has been made since the days of 'Struwwelpeter' (1845) and 'Max und Moritz' (1858). Information upon this point, and indeed upon the whole 'Jugendschriftenfrage,' may be found in Hermann L. Koester's 'Geschichte der deutschen Jugendliteratur' (Part I, Janssen, Hamburg, 1906, 2*s.* 6*d.* unbound; Part II, 1908, 2*s.* 6*d.*). Among the many modern picture-books the work of Ernst Kreidolf may be specially recommended. His 'Blumenmärchen' (2te Aufl., Schaffstein, Köln, 1*s.* 3*d.*) will appeal more to English children than even the famous 'Fitzebutze' (Schaffstein, Köln, 3*s.*), or the fantastic though poetic 'Schlafende Bäume' (Schaffstein, Köln, 2*s.*); while Gertrud und Walther Caspari's 'Kinderhumor für Auge und

Ohr' (Alfred Hahn, Leipzig, 1906, **2s.** 10**d.**) is delightfully bright in its colouring.

History and Geography.—Although German history and geography as such will hardly ever be taught in ordinary schools, a teacher of German should make it a point to be well informed as to the main facts of either subject, and should possess some standard German books with German names of places and events in his private library. The histories and atlases of this kind need not be very bulky and expensive: some really good German school and family books will amply suffice for his purpose. German books on German *Realien* do not seem to be as yet very familiar to English teachers of German. A few suggestions may therefore be welcome[1]. With regard to history, I can recommend David Müller's 'Leitfaden zur Geschichte des deutschen Volkes' (Berlin, [11] 1899, **2s.** 6**d.** cloth), the larger book by the same author, called 'Geschichte des deutschen Volkes in kurzgefasster übersichtlicher Darstellung' (Berlin, [18] 1902, 6**s.** bound). The 'Deutsche Geschichte' by O. Kämmel is also widely used in Germany. Some consider it to be now the best work of its kind (12**s.** 6**d.** half calf). A shorter work by Otto Kämmel also deserves to be recommended. It is called 'Der Werdegang des deutschen Volkes. Historische Richtlinien für gebildete Leser.' Vol. I. Das Mittelalter. Leipzig, 1896 (2**s.** 6**d.** cloth). Vol. II. Die Neuzeit. Leipzig, 1904 (3**s.** 6**d.** cloth). K. Biedermann's 'Deutsche Volks- und Kulturgeschichte für Schule und Haus,' 3 parts in 1 volume, Wiesbaden, [4] 1901 (7**s.** 6**d.** cloth), is much to be recommended. Teachers may like to read through Parts IV and V (on 'Deutsche Geschichte') of Friedrich Neubauer's 'Lehrbuch der Geschichte für höhere Lehranstalten,' 7th and 6th edd., Halle, 1905,

---

[1] In Germany an acquaintance with the principal English and French *Realien* is required by the present regulations of the *Oberlehrerprüfung* (see pp. 165 sqq.). There is so far no book on German *Realien* corresponding to Cl. Klöpper's *Englisches Real-Lexikon* and *Französisches Real-Lexikon*, or Langenscheidt's capital *Land und Leute in Frankreich* (*England*).

and consult J. Jastrow's book, 'Geschichte des deutschen Einheitstraumes und seiner Erfüllung' (Berlin, ⁴1891, 6s. unbound, 7s. half-bound). A useful 'Short history of Germany,' by Ernest F. Henderson, hails from America, New York, 1906 (10s. 6d.). Teachers who wish to read a masterly account of the course of universal history during the last four centuries cannot do better than read Dietrich Schäfer's 'Weltgeschichte der Neuzeit,' Berlin, 1907 (2 vols. bound 15s.). An excellent 'Atlas für Mittel- und Oberklassen höherer Lehranstalten' was published in 1898 at Bielefeld and Leipzig by R. Lehmann and W. Petzold (5s.). The small Atlas by E. Debes, 'Schulatlas für die mittlere Unterrichtsstufe,' Leipzig (1s. 6d.), will suffice for ordinary purposes. A useful little book is A. L. Hickmann, 'Geographisch-statischer Taschen-Atlas des deutschen Reiches.' 3 parts. Leipzig-Wien (2s. each part, cloth, or the three in one volume, 5s. cloth). There is a good 'Historischer Schulatlas' by F. W. Putzger (new ed. by Baldamus). Bielefeld and Leipzig, 1905 (2s. 10d. boards). Very cheap and admirable for class teaching is P. Knötel's 'Bilderatlas zur deutschen Geschichte' (with explanatory notes). Bielefeld and Leipzig, ³1903 (3s.). H. Luckenbach's cheap and excellent 'Abbildungen zur deutschen Geschichte' (München and Berlin, 1903, 1s. 6d. boards) may also be recommended. A book on Germany similar to G. Wendt's 'England' has still to be written[1], but a number of valuable books on German History and on German Life and Customs are enumerated in my 'Guide' on pp. 116 sqq. To these should now be added a small book by R. Kron, entitled, 'Bilder deutschen Lebens und Wesens; zusammenhängende Lesestoffe über Verhältnisse und Vorgänge des täglichen Lebens' (1905, 1s. 3d. cloth); Fr. Ratzel's 'Deutschland, Einführung in die Heimatkunde,' Leipzig (2s. 6d.); August Sach's 'Deutsche Heimat, Landschaft und Volkstum' (with excellent illustrations) (Halle, ²1902, 7s. 6d., 10s. cloth);

---

[1] In some ways the very useful and handy book, published by Messrs Teubner and written by many specialists, 'Von deutscher Art und Arbeit,' Vol. I, Leipzig, 1909 (5s. bound), will be found to render similar assistance.

Hans Meyer's ' Das deutsche Volkstum' (Leipzig-Wien, 1898, ²1903, 2 parts, in 1 or 2 vols. 9s. 6d. each, cloth); Georg Steinhausen's 'Geschichte der deutschen Kultur,' Leipzig-Wien, Bibliographisches Institut, 1904 (17s. bound); W. H. Dawson's 'German Life in Town and Country,' with illustrations from photographs (London, 1901, 3s. 6d. net); and 'Austrian Life,' London, 1904 (3s. 6d. net). Some older English books on Germany are W. H. Dawson, 'Germany and the Germans,' London, 1894, 2 vols. (26s.), and Sidney Whitman, 'Imperial Germany,' London, 1889 (new ed. 1895, 2s. 6d.). To these may be added the following recent books: H. Lichtenberger, 'L'Allemagne moderne,' Paris (3s. 3d.); O. Eltzbacher's 'Modern Germany,' London, 1905 (7s. 6d. net); W. H. Dawson's important 'Evolution of Modern Germany,' London, 1908 (£1. 1s. net); and also Mrs Alfred Sidgwick's interesting 'Home life in Germany,' 16 illustrations, London, 1908 (10s. 6d. net, bound). The work on 'The German Empire,' by Burt Estes Howard (New York, Macmillan Co., 1906, 8s. 6d. net), is good with regard to historical and constitutional questions, but does not deal with the intellectual aspects of Modern Germany. Concerning the rights and duties of German citizens, teachers will find reliable information in the book by A. Giese, 'Die deutsche Bürgerkunde,' Leipzig, ³1903 (1s. 6d. boards), and in G. Hoffmann and E. Groth, 'Deutsche Bürgerkunde, Kleines Handbuch des politisch Wissenswertesten für jedermann,' ³1902, Leipzig (2s. 6d. bound); A. Perls, 'Reichs- und Staats-Bürgerbuch,' Berlin (1s.); W. Griep, 'Bürgerkunde,' Leipzig, 1901 (2s. bound); W. Bazille, 'Unsre Reichsverfas- sung und deutsche Landesverfassungen,' Stuttgart, 1906 (2s.); W. Coermann, 'Die Reichsverfassung und Reichsverwaltung,' München, 1908 (1s. net).

General Information.—Succinct and reliable informa- tion on all matters connected with German history and biography, life and thought, may be obtained from Meyer's 'Kleines Konversations-Lexikon' in 3 volumes, 6th ed., Leipzig (half-bound, £1, 10s.), or from 'Der Kleine Brockhaus.'

another handy encyclopaedia in 2 vols., 1908 (bound £1. 4*s.*), either of which will prove of the greatest use and which every teacher of German should endeavour to get. John Wenzel's 'Comparative view of the executive and legislative departments of the governments of the United States, France, England and Germany' (Boston, U.S.A., 1901, 1*s.*) is also to be recommended. A concise book giving brief information concerning German affairs, institutions, customs, etc. is J. Kürschner's 'Jahrbuch,' published every year. Berlin-Leipzig-Eisenach (1*s.* unbound). Brief and reliable information concerning all living modern German literary men (not only poets and novelists), authors' societies, periodicals and newspapers is given in an annual publication called 'Deutscher Literatur-Kalender,' started by the late Joseph Kürschner. The 30th vol. appeared at Leipzig in 1908 (6*s.* 6*d.* bound), and there is now (since 1905) H. A. L. Degener's new annual 'Wer ist's? Zeitgenossenlexikon' (Vol. IV, Leipzig, 1908, 12*s.* 6*d.* cloth), corresponding to the English 'Who's Who?' and the new French 'Qui êtes-vous,' Paris, 1908, ²1909 (6*s.*).

Letters, Titles, Everyday etiquette.—Those who are anxious to obtain information about the right use of German titles and the proper way in which letters should be begun, ended and addressed, the manner in which titled persons should be spoken or written to, the best time for paying calls, and about those many details in which German customs differ from the English, may refer to J. von Eltz, 'Das goldene Anstandsbuch, ein Wegweiser für die gute Lebensart zu Hause, in Gesellschaft und im öffentlichen Leben,' Essen, ⁵1908 (5*s.* 6*d.*), and to Otto Friedrich Rammler, 'Deutscher Reichs-Universal-Briefsteller,' ed. by H. Th. Traut, Leipzig, 73rd edit. 1907 (3*s.* 9*d.*). Another useful English-German letter writer is the handy book by J. S. S. Rothwell, 'Deutsch-Englischer Briefsteller, Muster zu Briefen jeder Art, mit der gegenüberge-druckten englischen Übersetzung,' Stuttgart, Neff. No year. 4th ed. (4*s.* bound). A short book is Florian Lebrecht, 'Deutsche Familienbriefe zur Übung für Ausländer,' Breslau, 1906 (1*s.*).

Lessons may be made more interesting by the exhibition of picture post-cards, large and small, and by photographs of towns, scenery[1], monuments, great men, costumes, etc. Intending teachers and teachers travelling abroad should make a point of collecting such things and should bring back with them specimens of the coins, stamps, popular costumes, text, music and illustrations of the principal popular songs, and anything else characteristic of the places in which they have been. Such photographs and post-cards in so far as they would directly illustrate the authors read at school and modern German life in general should also at all good schools form part of the scholars' and of the teachers' reference libraries.

Method of Teaching.—However well informed a teacher may be, he will have to adapt himself in his teaching to the school curriculum, to the aims to be attained by his pupils, and he will have to give his most serious attention to the study and consideration of the methods to be followed in his teaching. No school teacher who takes the slightest interest in his subject can at the present time afford to keep aloof from the discussions as to the best method of teaching modern foreign languages, and every one will be able to learn a great deal from the books written on the subject of the teaching of German. A number of the most suggestive books have been enumerated on pp. 117—126. Some of these works a Modern Language teacher will no doubt wish to possess for himself, so as to be able to refer to them from time to time. The following books appear to me to be especially useful—W. H. Widgery, 'The teaching of languages in schools.' London, 1888, [2]1903 (1s.). W. Rippmann, 'Hints on teaching French' and 'Hints on teaching German.' See p. 122. Fr. Spencer, 'Aims

[1] In this connection I should like to point to the excellent series 'Land und Leute, Monographieen zur Erdkunde,' Bielefeld und Leipzig, Velhagen und Klasing, among which Professor Richard Linde's 'Lüneburger Heide' ([3]1907) and 'Niederelbe' ([2]1908) deserve special recommendation. The splendid photographs of German buildings and monuments published by the 'Neue Photographische Gesellschaft,' Aktien-Gesellschaft, Steglitz, near Berlin, will be found most useful.

and Practice of teaching.' Cambridge, 1897 (6s.). An interesting account of the new methods of Modern Language teaching in some particularly good German schools was given by Miss M. Brebner in her pamphlet called 'The Method of teaching Modern Languages in Germany.' London, 1898 (1s. 6d. cloth). All of these books advocate more or less the so-called Reformmethode or 'Neuere Richtung,' and are therefore in accordance with the requirements of the 'Kaiserliche Erlass' (Kiel, Nov. 26th, 1900), which determined among other things that teachers of modern languages should especially strive to give their pupils facility in speaking in the foreign tongue and the ability clearly to understand current authors. Most of them also lay stress on the value of modern languages as humanistic studies—a consideration which should be always kept in view. In this connection Otto Siepmann's lectures may again be mentioned. His views on this point are sound and forcibly expressed, and I am in hearty agreement with him when he discusses the spirit in which modern languages should be taught. Similar views are expressed by Ch. Sigwalt (see page 123). The books and pamphlets that have so far been mentioned are written for teachers whose native tongue is *not* German, but much that is useful can also be learned from some German books for German teachers, if one bears in mind that the standards set up in them require modification and abatement, as German is a foreign language in this country. Teachers can still learn a great deal from a careful study of the books by E. Laas and R. Hildebrand (see my 'Guide,' pp. 37 and 119, 120), but generally speaking they will derive most benefit from the works by R. Lehmann, 'Der deutsche Unterricht, eine Methodik für höhere Lehranstalten,' Berlin, ²1897 (9s. cloth), and by G. Wendt, 'Der deutsche Unterricht,' München, 1896 (3s. 6d.). See p. 126. The latter contains also an admirable bibliography. More recent is Lehmann's 'Der Unterricht im Deutschen,' contributed to W. Lexis' splendid work 'Die Reform des höheren Schulwesens in Preussen,'

Halle, 1902, pp. 177—190. The most comprehensive work on the subject, mainly intended for Germans, will be the encyclo paedia edited by Adolf Matthias which is mentioned on p. 131.

Valuable works on German education in general, and therefore including the teaching of modern languages, are : James E. Russell, 'German Higher Schools. The History, Organization and Method of Secondary Education in Germany' (New York, 1899, 7s. 6d. net). E. M. Sadler, 'Problems in Prussian Secondary Education for Boys, with special reference to similar questions in England' (London, 1898). F. E. Bolton, 'The Secondary School System of Germany' (London, 1900, 6s. 6d.). W. H. Winch, 'Notes on German Schools, with special relation to curriculum and methods of teaching' (London, 1904, 6s.). Hugo Müller, 'Das höhere Schulwesen Deutschlands am Anfang des 20. Jahrhunderts' (Stuttgart, 1904, 2s. unbound). See also Baumeister's Handbuch, Vol. I. 2. Friedrich Paulsen's fine little book 'Das deutsche Bildungswesen in seiner geschichtlichen Entwickelung,' Leipzig, 1906 (published in Teubner's excellent popular series 'Aus Natur und Geisteswelt,' No. 100), has just been well translated by Theodor Lorenz under the title 'German Education Past and Present,' London, 1908 (5s. bound). The learned translator has prefixed a useful chapter of terminological notes in which all the technical terms of German education are either translated into English or discussed and explained. On 'German ideals of to-day' in life and education there is a recent thoughtful article by Kuno Francke in 'The Atlantic Monthly' of Dec. 1905 (1s.) which deserves careful perusal by anyone who takes an interest in the intellectual life of Germany. It has been reprinted in his book 'German ideals of to-day and other essays on German culture,' Boston and New York, 1907 (6s. 3d.).

Concerning higher and highest German education teachers will find valuable information in Fr. Paulsen, 'Die Deutsche Universität als Unterrichtsanstalt und als Werkstätte der wissenschaftlichen Forschung' (in 'Deutsche Rundschau,'

xx. Heft 12, Sept. 1894, pp. 341 ff.); 'Die höheren Schulen und das Universitätsstudium im 20sten Jahrhundert' (Braunschweig, 1901, 10*d.*); 'Die deutschen Universitäten und das Universitätsstudium' (a fine book, Berlin, 1902, 7*s.* 3*d.* bound)[1]; 'Die höheren Schulen Deutschlands und ihr Lehrerstand, in ihrem Verhältnis zum Staat und zur geistigen Kultur,' Braunschweig, 1904, 6*d.* (all by the same author). The following volumes (10*d.* each) of the 'Sammlung Göschen' deserve to be warmly recommended: Paul Stoetzner, 'Das öffentliche Unterrichtswesen Deutschlands in der Gegenwart,' Leipzig, 1901, and Friedrich Seiler, 'Geschichte des deutschen Unterrichtswesens,' Leipzig, 1906. (Vol. 1 to the end of the 18th cent., Vol. 11 till the present day.) In both of these works the best books of reference for a more detailed study are carefully enumerated.

With regard to French methods, which teachers of German may wish to compare, refer to 'Special Reports on Education in France,' London, 1899 (a reprint from Vol. 11 of 'Special Reports' of the Education Department), and to Oskar Mey's 'Frankreichs Schulen in ihrem organischen Bau und ihrer historischen Entwickelung, mit Berücksichtigung der neuesten Reformen.' 2nd ed. (rewritten and enlarged). Leipzig, 1901 (4*s.* 10*d.* unbound). See also the account given by Eugène Stropeno in Baumeister's 'Handbuch der Erziehungs- und Unterrichtslehre für höhere Schulen,' Vol. 1. Part 2 (München, 1897), pp. 419—461, and also pp. 737—892, where the organisation of secondary education in Great Britain has been treated by me at length, and has in some places been compared with the conditions obtaining in Germany.

Teachers should also make it a point to read some of the

---

[1] An English translation of this important book has recently been published by Messrs Longmans, Green and Co. (London, 1906, bound, 15*s.* net). The translation is by Frank Thilly and William W. Elwang, to which is prefixed a very valuable preface by M. E. Sadler, and another suggestive preface by one of the American translators (Thilly).

periodicals enumerated in section 1 of the bibliographical appendix to this book, such as ' Modern Language Teaching,' 'Modern Language Review,' 'Die Neueren Sprachen,' 'Archiv für das Studium der Neueren Sprachen und Litteraturen,' ' Les Langues Modernes, Bulletin Mensuel de la société des professeurs de langues vivantes,' ' Modern Language Notes,' in order to keep themselves in touch with modern theories and opinions on questions of the method and practice of teaching. Some of these ought to be taken in by the better schools for the teachers' reference library.

I trust that the recommendations and hints given above may enable teachers to make a good choice of books of reference in the various departments of their teaching and private study. More than once I have been privately asked by practical teachers for information of this kind; may the suggestions and recommendations now given be found useful to a wider circle of readers, and thus render some service to the cause of the study and teaching of German in Great Britain!

APPENDIX

EXTRACT from the Ordnung der Prüfung für das
Lehramt an höheren Schulen in Preußen vom 12.
September 1898. Halle a. S. ³1906.

§ 8.
Umfang und Form der Prüfung.

Die Prüfung besteht aus zwei Teilen, der Allgemeinen und der
Fachprüfung. Beide sind schriftlich und mündlich; die schriftlichen Hausarbeiten sind vor der mündlichen Prüfung zu erledigen.

Sowohl in der Allgemeinen als auch in der Fachprüfung ist dem
Unterrichtsbedürfnisse der höheren Schulen Rechnung zu tragen.

§ 9.
Prüfungsgegenstände.

1. Prüfungsgegenstände sind

A. in der Allgemeinen Prüfung für jeden Kandidaten : Philosophie, Pädagogik und deutsche Literatur; ferner für die Kandidaten, welche einer der christlichen Kirchen angehören: Religionslehre.

[In den von den Kandidaten gewählten Fächern (in der Fachprüfung) muß sich im allgemeinen Französisch mit Englisch ver-
binden, aber es kann an Stelle der einen oder der andern Fremdsprache auch Deutsch von den Kandidaten gewählt werden. K. B.]

§ 10.

*Maß der in der allgemeinen Prüfung zu stellenden
Anforderungen.*

Bei der Allgemeinen Prüfung kommt es nicht auf die Darlegung
fachmännischer Kenntnisse an, sondern auf den Nachweis der von
Lehrern höherer Schulen zu fordernden allgemeinen Bildung auf
den betreffenden Gebieten.

Demnach hat der Kandidat in der ihm nach § 28, 1 obliegenden
Hausarbeit nicht bloß ausreichendes Wissen und ein verständnis-
volles Urteil über den behandelten Gegenstand zu bekunden,
sondern auch zu zeigen, daß er einer sprachrichtigen, logisch
geordneten, klaren und hinlänglich gewandten Darstellung fähig
ist.

Für die *mündliche* Prüfung ist zu fordern, daß der Kandidat

1. in der Religionslehre sich mit Inhalt und Zusammenhang
der Heiligen Schrift bekannt zeigt, einen allgemeinen Überblick
über die Geschichte der christlichen Kirche hat und die Hauptlehren seiner Konfession kennt;

2. in der Philosophie mit den wichtigsten Tatsachen ihrer
Geschichte sowie mit den Hauptlehren der Logik und der Psychologie bekannt ist, auch eine bedeutendere philosophische Schrift
mit Verständnis gelesen hat;

3. in der Pädagogik nachweist, daß er ihre philosophischen
Grundlagen sowie die wichtigsten Erscheinungen in ihrer Entwickelung seit dem 16. Jahrhundert kennt und bereits einiges Verständnis für die Aufgaben seines künftigen Berufes gewonnen hat;

4. in der deutschen Literatur dartut, daß ihm deren allgemeiner Entwickelungsgang, namentlich seit dem Beginne ihrer
Blüteperiode im 18. Jahrhundert, bekannt ist, und daß er auch
nach dem Abgange von der Schule zu seiner weiteren Fortbildung
bedeutendere Werke dieser Zeit mit Verständnis gelesen hat.

§ 11 bis § 27.

Maß der in der Fachprüfung zu stellenden Anforderungen.

Vorbemerkung. Auf jedem Prüfungsgebiete ist von den
Kandidaten Bekanntschaft mit den wichtigsten wissenschaftlichen
Hilfsmitteln zu fordern.

§ 11.

Abstufung der Lehrbefähigung.

1. Die Lehrbefähigung in den einzelnen Fächern hat zwei Stufen : die eine, für die unteren und mittleren Klassen (zweite Stufe), reicht bis Untersekunda einschließlich, die andere (erste Stufe) umfaßt auch die oberen Klassen bis Oberprima einschließlich.

3. Bei der Erwerbung der Lehrbefähigung für die erste Stufe ist in jedem Falle Voraussetzung, daß den für die zweite Stufe in dem betreffenden Fache zu stellenden Forderungen entsprochen ist.

§ 14.

Deutsch.

Von Kandidaten, welche die Befähigung für den *deutschen Unterricht* nachweisen wollen, ist zu fordern

a. für die *zweite Stufe* : Sichere Kenntnis der neuhochdeutschen Elementargrammatik und Bekanntschaft mit der Geschichte der neuhochdeutschen Schriftsprache ; eingehendere Beschäftigung mit klassischen Werken der neueren Literatur, insbesondere aus ihren für die Jugendbildung verwendbaren Gebieten, und Übersicht über den Entwickelungsgang der neuhochdeutschen Literatur. Außerdem ist Bekanntschaft mit den Grundzügen der Rhetorik, Poetik und Metrik sowie mit den für die Schule wichtigen antiken und germanischen Sagen darzutun ;

b. für die *erste Stufe* überdies : Eine Beherrschung des Mittelhochdeutschen, welche befähigt, leichtere Werke ohne Schwierigkeit zu lesen und mit grammatischer und lexikalischer Genauigkeit zu erklären ; eine, wenigstens für die mittelhochdeutsche und neuere Zeit, auf ausgedehnterer Lektüre beruhende Kenntnis des Entwickelungsganges der gesamten deutschen Literatur ; Vertrautheit mit der Poetik und deutschen Metrik sowie mit denjenigen Lehren der Rhetorik, deren Kenntnis für die Anleitung zur Anfertigung deutscher Aufsätze in den oberen

Klassen erforderlich ist; dazu nach Wahl des Kandidaten *entweder* Bekanntschaft mit den Hauptergebnissen der historischen Grammatik und Kenntnis der Elemente des Gotischen und Althochdeutschen, *oder* die Lehrbefähigung in der Philosophischen Propädeutik (§ 13).

§ 17.

Französisch.

Von den Kandidaten, welche die Lehrbefähigung im *Französischen* nachweisen wollen, ist zu fordern, daß sie Kenntnis der lateinischen Elementargrammatik nachweisen nebst der Fähigkeit, einfache Schulschriftsteller, wie Cäsar, wenigstens in leichteren Stellen, richtig aufzufassen und zu übersetzen ; sodann

a. für die *zweite Stufe* : Kenntnis der Elemente der Phonetik, richtige und zu fester Gewöhnung gebrachte Aussprache; Vertrautheit mit der Formenlehre und Syntax sowie der elementaren Synonymik ; Besitz eines ausreichenden Schatzes an Worten und Wendungen und einige Übung im mündlichen Gebrauche der Sprache ; Einsicht in den neufranzösischen Versbau und Übersicht über den Entwickelungsgang der französischen Literatur seit dem 17. Jahrhundert, aus welcher einige Werke der hervorragendsten Dichter und Prosaiker, auch der neuesten Zeit, mit Verständnis gelesen sein müssen ; Fähigkeit zu sicherer Übersetzung der gewöhnlichen Schriftsteller ins Deutsche und zu einer von gröberen sprachlich-stilistischen Verstößen freien schriftlichen Darstellung in der fremden Sprache ;

b. für die *erste Stufe* : Für den schriftlichen und mündlichen Gebrauch der Sprache nicht bloß volle grammatische Sicherheit bei wissenschaftlicher Begründung der grammatischen Kenntnisse, sondern auch umfassendere Vertrautheit mit dem Sprachschatz und der Eigentümlichkeit des Ausdrucks, sowie eine für alle Unterrichtszwecke ausreichende Gewandtheit in dessen Handhabung ; übersichtliche Kenntnis der geschichtlichen Entwickelung der Sprache seit ihrem Hervorgehen aus dem Lateinischen, ferner Kenntnis der allgemeinen Entwickelung der französischen Literatur, verbunden mit eingehender Lektüre einiger hervorragender Schriftwerke aus früheren Perioden wie aus der Gegenwart ; Einsicht in die Gesetze des französischen Versbaues älterer und neuerer Zeit; Bekanntschaft mit der Geschichte Frankreichs, soweit sie für die sachliche Erläuterung der gebräuchlichen Schulschriftsteller erforderlich ist.

Bemerkung. Für minder eingehende Kenntnisse auf dem Gebiete der geschichtlichen Entwickelung der Sprache kann eine besonders tüchtige Kenntnis der neueren Literatur nebst hervorragender Beherrschung der gegenwärtigen Sprache ausgleichend eintreten.

§ 18.

Englisch.

Von den Kandidaten, welche die Lehrbefähigung im *Englischen* nachweisen wollen, ist zu fordern, daß sie Kenntnis der lateinischen Elementargrammatik nachweisen nebst der Fähigkeit, einfache Schulschriftsteller, wie Cäsar, wenigstens in leichteren Stellen, richtig aufzufassen und zu übersetzen; sodann

a. für die *zweite Stufe*: Kenntnis der Elemente der Phonetik, richtige und zu fester Gewöhnung gebrachte Aussprache: Vertrautheit mit der Formenlehre und Syntax sowie der elementaren Synonymik; Besitz eines ausreichenden Schatzes an Worten und Wendungen und einige Übung im mündlichen Gebrauche der Sprache; Übersicht über den Entwickelungsgang der englischen Literatur seit Shakespeare, aus welcher einige Werke der hervorragendsten Dichter und Prosaiker, auch der neuesten Zeit, mit Verständnis gelesen sein müssen; Fähigkeit zu sicherer Übersetzung der gewöhnlichen Schriftsteller ins Deutsche und zu einer von gröberen sprachlich-stilistischen Verstößen freien schriftlichen Darstellung in der fremden Sprache;

b. für die *erste Stufe*: Für den schriftlichen und mündlichen Gebrauch der Sprache nicht bloß volle grammatische Sicherheit bei wissenschaftlicher Begründung der grammatischen Kenntnisse, sondern auch umfassendere Vertrautheit mit dem Sprachschatz und der Eigentümlichkeit des Ausdrucks, sowie eine für alle Unterrichtszwecke ausreichende Gewandtheit in dessen Handhabung; übersichtliche Kenntnis der geschichtlichen Entwickelung der Sprache von der altenglischen Periode an; Kenntnis der allgemeinen Entwickelung der Literatur, verbunden mit eingehender Lektüre einiger hervorragender Schriftwerke aus früheren Perioden wie aus der Gegenwart; Einsicht in die Gesetze des englischen Versbaues älterer und neuerer Zeit; Bekanntschaft mit der Geschichte Englands, soweit sie für die sachliche Erläuterung der gebräuchlichen Schulschriftsteller erforderlich ist.

Bemerkung. Für minder eingehende Kenntnisse auf dem Gebiete der geschichtlichen Entwickelung der Sprache kann eine besonders tüchtige Kenntnis der neueren Literatur nebst hervorragender Beherrschung der gegenwärtigen Sprache ausgleichend eintreten.

§ 28.

Schriftliche Hausarbeiten.

2. Prüfungsarbeiten aus dem Gebiete der klassischen Philologie sind in lateinischer, aus dem der neueren Sprachen in der betreffenden Sprache, alle übrigen aber in deutscher Sprache abzufassen.

§ 33.

Ausführung der mündlichen Prüfung.

5. Die Fachprüfung im Französischen, Englischen, Polnischen oder Dänischen ist insoweit in der betreffenden Sprache selbst zu führen, daß dadurch die Fertigkeit des Kandidaten im mündlichen Gebrauche derselben ermittelt wird.

CONTINENTAL TRAINING FOR TEACHERS.

The following communication has been issued by the Board of Education :

The French and Prussian Governments have initiated, in conjunction with the Board of Education, a scheme whereby a number of young teachers (men and women) can be appointed as temporary "assistants" for one year in French lycées and collèges or Prussian gymnasia respectively. The two Ministries will proceed shortly to make fresh appointments.

The main duty of the "assistant" will be to conduct small conversation classes for about two hours daily.

Though not taking any part in the regular instruction of pupils, he will, both in France and Germany, be considered in all other respects as the colleague of the masters. He will not receive a salary, but he will be lodged and boarded at the institution to which he is attached, subject to the provision that in Germany, in certain cases, a sum of about £65 (1,300 marks) may be paid to him in lieu of board and lodging.

Candidates for such posts must be teachers (or intending teachers) in secondary schools, and should preferably be graduates of some British university. Applications, containing particulars as to course of study and qualifications, should be forwarded without delay to the Director of Special Inquiries and Reports, Board of Education Library, St Stephen's House, Cannon-row, Westminster, with testimonials in duplicate as to character and capacity and teaching experience, and a medical certificate of health. It will also be necessary for each candidate to have a personal interview with the Director at his office.

LES NOUVELLES INSTRUCTIONS OFFICIELLES RELATIVES À L'ENSEIGNEMENT DES LANGUES VIVANTES EN FRANCE.

See Mr G. Delobel's article in *Modern Language Teaching*, Vol. v (April, 1909), 78—81.

INDEX

Abbreviations, the chief German, 46
Aims of Modern Language Teaching
    in Secondary Schools, 10, 13,
    44, 49, 59, 60, 62, 89
Alliteration, 95
Analytic method, 3
Answers, in complete sentences, 35

Bibliographical appendix, 114–128
    periodicals, 113–6
    reports, 116–7
    books, pamphlets and essays on
      modern language teaching,
      117 sqq.
    books on teaching of German,
      126
    books on phonetics, 127–8
Books of courtesy, 1
Books on the study and teaching of
    German, 129–164

Cambridge Medieval and Modern
    Languages Tripos, 42, 105
Classics, study of the, 26, 43, 46–51
    canon of suitable books to be
      read, 43–4, 46–7
    canon of suitable pieces to be
      learnt by heart, 47
    rimes in classics, 23
    annotated editions of classics,
      26, 44
    biographical accounts of classics,
      58–9
    English renderings of foreign
      classics, 54

Classics
    French and German 17th and
      18th cent. classics, 49–50
    German classics, 149–151
Class-rooms, special, to be allotted
    to modern language teaching, 5
Coins, foreign, 32, 45, 160
Composition, ordinary, only to be
    done by advanced pupils, 14
Composition, original, 14, 57, 143
Conversation, 34–40, 142–3
Correspondence, international, 16,
    108

Dialects, 66–7, 97
Dictation, 21, 24, 97
Dictionaries, 131–5
    German, 131 sqq.
    German-English, 131–3
    German-German, 133–4
    of doubtful points, 137
    of foreign words in German, 134
    etymological, 134
    orthographical, 139
    of quotations, 135
    synonymical, 134
    systematic English-German, 134–
      5
    for travelling, 42, 133
    commercial and miscellaneous,
      135
Differences between German and
    English, 62
Difficulties (chief) of German
    Grammar, 78–81

Difficulties (chief) of German pronunciation, 69–75
Direct method of teaching modern languages, 3, 34–7

English too much neglected in many schools, 56, 58
Essays, books on German essay writing, 143
Etymological comparison, 33, 92–3, 134
Examinations
  drawbacks of set books in, 48–9
  foreign, for mod. lang. teachers, 35–6, 165 sqq.
  neglect of the spoken language in, 5
  viva voce, 35–6, 48
Exchange of
  lessons, 108
  letters, 15–16, 108
  pupils, 16
  teachers, 39–40, 170–1
Explanation of poems, dramas, etc., 56–8

Ferienkurse, 40–1
Foreign words in German, books on, 134
Form association, 29, 77
Form, metrical, 54–6
Fraktur, 64–5
French
  difficult sounds, 18, 19
  enunciation, 20
  first teaching of, 34
  metre, 23, 54
  relation to English, 29

Geography, 88, 100, 109, 156–7
German
  adjectives, 79
  aim of teaching, 62
  books on teaching, 126, 131–164
  classics (books on teaching), 146 sqq.
  conversation, 34–7, 142–3
  dialects, 66–7, 97
  dictionaries, 131–5
  difficulties of, 69–75, 78–81

German
  essays, 57, 143
  first teaching of, 34
  genders, 81–2
  geography, 88, 156–7
  grammar teaching, 13–14, 25–9, 75–81
  grammars, 135–140
  handwriting, 63–4, 140
  history, 88, 156–8
  idioms, 11, 30, 142–3
  language (books on history of), 138–9
  letters, use of, 62–5, 93, 140
  letter writing, 15, 46
  literature (books on history of), 144–7
  literature, should it be taught as such? 58
  lyrics, 150–1
  metre, 54–6, 78, 148
  middle high German, 87, 94, 153
  mythology and sagas, 153
  names, 43, 84
  old German, 151
  old high German, 87, 89
  picture books, 155
  punctuation, 25, 140
  reader, 43–6
  'Realien,' 32, 43, 45–6, 88
  sixteenth century, 152
  spelling, 24–5, 55, 139–140
  syntax, 80, 92; books on, 137
  titles, 159
  word formation, 83–4
Glottal stop, 19, 71
Gradation of reading, 42–4
  of poems learnt by heart, 47–8
Grammars, German, 135–140
  defects of existing school grammars, 27, 76
Grammar teaching, 13, 25–9, 75 sqq.
Gramophone, 21, 67

Handwriting (German), 63–4, 140
Historical Grammar, 26, 29, 83, 91–3
History, 88, 100, 109, 156–7
Holiday courses for teachers and students, 40–1

Idioms, to be taught, 11, 30
   explained (books on), 142-3
Illustrated Reader, 43-6
   Primer, 43
Information, general information
   about Germany, 158-9
Institute for foreign language
   teachers, 110
International correspondence, 15-16
Intonation, characteristic foreign, to
   be taught, 20-1, 67

Latin words in German, French or
   English, 29
Learning by heart, 47-8, 53
Leave of absence for mod. lang.
   teachers, 38
Letters and sounds, 18-19, 93
Letters in German reader, 46
Letter writing, 15, 32, 46
Library of mod. lang. books for
   junior and senior pupils, 6,
   50-1; mod. lang. students'
   reference library, 107; ideal
   teachers' library, 129-164
Literature, foreign, should it be
   taught in schools, 58; English
   literature, 56, 58
   books on German, 144-7

Maps, 5, 43, 45
Method of reading with a class,
   51-8
Methodical preparation of lessons,
   51-2
Metre, study of, 54-6
   books on German, 148
Modern Languages
   Association, 38, 108, 113
   at Cambridge, 36, 42
   classes, 5-6
   educational value of, 4, 60
   connected with English, 10-11
   connected with study of History
     and Geography, 11, 88
   interest in, 44, 59
   not to be degraded, 60
   not to be taught like classical
     languages, 10

Modern Languages
   to be taught mainly by English
     men and women, 41
   how the teaching of them may
     be improved, 4-6
   time allotted to them in schools,
     4, 46
   principles of teaching, 9-11
   methods of teaching, 7
   books on methods of teaching,
     117-126, 160-4
   onesidedness of some methods of
     teaching, 7-8
   the direct or analytic method of
     teaching, 3
   general agreement as to method
     of teaching, 9
   periodicals, 114-116
   scholarships, 101-2, 151-3
Mother tongue, sound teaching of it
   important for foreign language
   teaching, 56
Mots populaires and Mots savants,
   29, 77, 101

Names, German geographical, 43
   proper and family, 84
'Neuere Richtung,' 3, 21, 160

Object lessons, 42
Old German, study of, 94, 101-2,
   151-3
Oral test in examinations, 5, 35-6,
   48
Orthography, German, 24-5, 65,
   139-140

Paraphrase, 15, 53
Periodicals, 114-116
Phonetics, 17-20, 97-9
Phonetics (drill in), 11
   (books on), 127-8, 141-2
Phonetic transcription, 21-3, 44, 69,
   141
Phonograph, 21, 48, 53, 67, 119,
   122
Phrases (idiomatic), 11, 30, 142-3
Pictures (use of) in lower forms, 31,
   34, 36-7
   in Reader, 43-5

Picture Books, 155
Picture Post Cards, 32, 112, 160
Plays, discussion of great, 54–8
    historical, 58
    acted abroad, 57
    classical (books on), 148–9
Poems to be learnt by heart, 47–8,
    53
    to be read in school, 52
Poetic licence, 55, 78
Poetry, books on the theory of,
    148–9
Precision, 67
Prefixes, 84
Prepositions, use of German, 78
    origin of certain German, 77
Prescribed books in examinations,
    48–9
Primer, 43
Pronunciation, 11, 17–21
    German, 17–20, 66–75, 87, 93–4,
    97–9, 140–2
    of Goethe and Schiller, 23, 73–4
    of certain French words, 18–19, 23
Punctuation, 25
    book on German p., 140

Reader, centre of mod. lang.
    teaching, 43
    what to reject and what to
    include in it, 44–6
Reading, to be placed in the fore-
    front, 13
    method of reading with a class,
    51–8
    lesson, preparation of teacher
    for, 51–2
Readings and recitations by foreign-
    ers, 68
'Realien,' 32, 43, 45–6, 88, 108–9,
    154–160
Reciting, 20, 47, 68
Reform movement, 2
Relation of French and German to
    English, 29
Reproductions, 15
Residence abroad, 38–42, 109–112,
    160
Results of teaching mod. langs.,
    59–60

Rimes in the classics, 23, 56

Self-abnegation of teacher, 52
Series method, 31–2, 120
Size of classes, 5
Sounds
    sound charts, 17, 68
    sounds and letters, 18–19, 93
    etymological   correspondences
    between English and German
    sounds, 29, 33
Spelling, 21, 24–5, 65, 93
    new German, 65–6, 93, 139–140
Spoken language often neglected in
    examinations, 5, 35–6, 48
Sprachgefühl, 14, 28
Structure of Dramas, books on,
    148
    of dramas to be explained, 56–8
Study of German (what it comprises),
    87–8

Tables of foreign moneys, weights,
    measures, etc., 32, 45
Teachers of foreign languages, only
    duly qualified ones to be ap-
    pointed, 5
    qualifications of, 9, 86–8, 117
    scholarships for, 38–9
    exchange of, 39, 170–1
    to be mainly English, 41
    residence abroad of, 38–41, 109–
    112, 160
    number of hours they should be
    required to teach, 10
    of German, ideal reference
    library for, 129–164
    training of, 5, 9, 86–113, 117
    training of, at school, 99–103
    training of, at the University,
    103–7
    training of, after the University
    course, 107–113
    training of, abroad, 109–113
Theatre, 57–8
Theory of poetry (books on), 148
Time, all important for success in
    mod. lang. teaching, 4
Titles, 46, 159
Translation, 13, 50, 54

Travelling Scholarships for teachers and students needed, 38–9
    at Birmingham, 39

University training in modern languages, 103–7
Use of German type, 64–5
Utilitarian views on mod. lang. study, 49–50, 60

Verbs, strong, 79
    reflexive, 79–80

Verbs, separable, 80
Versification, oldest German, 95
Vocabulary, methods of increasing, 11, 31–4
Vowels, modified, 24, 65, 79

Wall-maps of foreign countries, 5, 43, 45
Wall-pictures, 31–2, 34, 36, 155
Word formation, 33, 83–4

Young, books for the, 154–5

Secretaries of

        The Modern Language Association, p. 113

        The International Phonetic Association, p. 116

        The Simplified Spelling Society, p. 139

        The English Goethe Society, p. 62

        The Allgemeiner Deutscher Sprachverein, p. 62

www.ingramcontent.com/pod-product-compliance
Ingram Content Group UK Ltd.
Pitfield, Milton Keynes, MK11 3LW, UK
UKHW012328130625
459647UK00009B/128